Everybody Sells

Escape from Mediocrity, Close Every One of your Sales, and Live an Epic Life

Written by Cris Urzua

www.crisurzua.com

www.mindsetandskills.com

www.sellingthroughservice.com

#EverybodySells

© Cris Urzua 2015

Translated by Matthew James Roudebush

Contact@MJRLanguages.com
Facebook.com/MJRLanguage
www.MJRLanguages.com

ACKNOWLEDGEMENTS

Gratitude is not a mere *"thank you,"* nor is it an *"I appreciate it"* to the person who occasionally helps you out. It's the noblest way to live life.

Thank you to my parents for selling me the ideas and dreams that have raised me to be just as I am, to my brother for following up on my inner child, and to Laura, my girlfriend, for allowing me to sell myself everyday as the best life partner.

Thank you to my customers for your trust and support, and thank you to the internet for allowing me to knock on the door of 100,000 people in 36 hours and to start a life anew, teaching what I know how to do best:

Selling.

And thanks to myself for being obsessive.

I love you all,

Cris Urzua

Table of Contents

Stage 1: Introduction to Chaos
(Have you got what it takes to sell?)

*	WARNING: Read this before moving on
*	This Book's Backbone
1	Capital Reality and Base Reality: Your Safety Net
2	Your Relationship with Money
3	The Sacred Trinity of "Get Rich"
4	Salespeople Make the World Go Round
5	Your Personal Definition of Success
6	The Pianist (The Bad Reputation of Sales)
7	Less Hawaiian Shirts, More Well-Tailored Suits
8	The 5 Hawaiian Shirt Mistakes
9	The Future of Sales
10	6 Things You NEED to Know Before Getting into Sales
11	The Manifest

Stage 2: The Mindset of a Salesman
(Understand yourself, to Sell to Them)

12	The Key: The Space between Your Ears
13	Open Mind, Closed Mouth
14	Selective Deafness
15	Justification: Human Nature (Say No to Conformism)
16	The Biggest Mistake: Underestimation
17	Ethics of a Salesman
18	Neurosis: Nothing Is by Chance
19	Dress for Success: How You Look Is How You Are Treated
20	Your Body Language
21	Motivation
22	Life Vision and Goals

Stage 3: Your Customer's Mindset
(Understanding their Mind and Closing the Sale)

23	80% Human, 20% product
24	Communicating with Your Customer (Filters)
25	Emotional Purchases, Logical Justifications
26	VISUALS: Don't tell them, show them
27	Your Customer's EGO
28	Fear of Losing (Loss Aversion)
29	Need for Closu-
30	Your Customer Wants What They Don't Have and What They Admire
31	The Value of a Referral
32	Faster Horses
33	AGREE: Your Customer Is Right (Even If They Aren't)
34	Got Haters?
35	We Hate to Be Sold, But We Love to Buy
36	Weakness to Opportunity
37	Best-Selling Emotions
38	How to Give Advice that Goes Somewhere
39	Objections and How to Defeat Them
40	Rejection: Your Feelings to the Blender
41	The Most Important Part of a Sale
*	Who is Cris Urzua
*	Glossary

WARNING!

STOP!

This is the most important part of this book.

If you don't read this explanation carefully, you risk not even understanding a bit of this book's content, and I can't let that happen. I can't let you waste the most valuable non-renewable resource that you have: **Your time!**

The following book is not just a book to *"learn how to sell."* It's not just a *"guide"* or a *"manual."* It's not just *"tips"* and *"strategies"* to manipulate people and make them do what you say…

NO! It's not just that.

The following book is an explanation of life.

It's a twisted and efficient explanation of the adventure of living the life of a salesman. The life of someone who recognizes the power of their voice and their existence. Of someone who is neurotic and dares to take control over their own ship and that bets on themselves every day that they'll reach their desired outcomes.

This book seeks to alter your life philosophy. It seeks to dismantle the four walls of your thought process and to expose you to the incredible potential within human beings who break free of excuses, false beliefs, and lies crafted by their own minds.

This book is a tribute to all of us that make our country's economy go round. To all of us that wake up at 4 o'clock in the morning to squeeze those extra 3 hours out of the day. To those of us who, by looking in the mirror, get all the motivation necessary to get up again after falling down a hundred times.

This book goes out to everyone who embraces selling as if it were as vital as breathing.

This book is for everyone who filters out the NO's and builds up the YES's.

This book is your new bible on finance.

This book is a mirror image of each one of us.

And now, with the sole objective of saving you time and steering you in the right direction, I've also got to clarify who this book is NOT for.

This book is NOT for:

- Whoever wants to be a millionaire in 5 minutes working from home.

- Whoever thinks that lying is a part of a sales process.

- Whoever thinks they already have and know everything.

- Whoever thinks investing time and money in their growth is not worth it.

- People whose idea of a great weekend is watching "Jersey shore."

- And definitely, this book is NOT for people that are just going to read it.

This book is for those who will take action.

Remember that knowledge is just potential power!

Knowledge combined with action is what grants true power!

Therefore, don't waste your time reading this book if you don't plan on applying even a bit of what you read. Please don't waste your time. This book will be very exciting for a brief moment, but if you don't apply anything, you'll fall right back into that little cycle of self-sabotage and excuses about why you don't have the life that you want.

Don't waste your time. Go back to your routine and keep doing what you've been doing up until now.

<u>It's too easy to have an average life.</u>

<u>It's hard to sell and negotiate yourself the life you deserve.</u>

See you on the other side,

Cris Urzua

THIS BOOK'S BACKBONE

"An ounce of action is worth a ton of theory"
-Ralph Waldo Emerson

It's great that you're still here! If you're still excited about the idea of taking action and reading this book to learn how to sell like a pro, I need to explain its structure and the instructions you'll need to follow to maximize what you learn.

This book's backbone: TAKING ACTION.

Every chapter is carefully designed to motivate you to take action. There's no point to reading all the incredible content if you don't practice it, if you don't truly motivate yourself to put it into practice. Don't be afraid to scratch this book, to bend the pages, to scribble down in them, and to tear them up!

In order to help you along this path and give you the necessary push so that when you finish this book you're a completely different salesman, you'll find two sections at the end (or middle) of each chapter:

1)   RECAP
2)   ACTION

In **RECAP**, you'll get the whole chapter's Kobe Beef, meaning the most important points 100% summarized for easy digestion. This is the content you'll want to post on Twitter, on Facebook, and on all your social networks to start getting out of the salesman closet and to position yourself as an expert in the field. This is the juicy part of each chapter. Don't forget to tag me and use the hashtag #EverybodySells so our entire community can see you!

In **ACTION**, you'll find a <u>mandatory</u> exercise if you're concerned about growing as a salesman. If you don't do these exercises, you might as well throw the book out the window and never open it again. They are simple, easy, and fun. Some are uncomfortable, some will scare you, and some will make you question things you previously didn't know.

But all of them, every single one of them, will help you grow as a person and as a salesman.
In several chapters you'll find a section called **GOODIES**, which is basically a section that has a few freebies for you.

Every GOODIE is a completely free online tool that you can download to help you along the course of the book.

The time is now!

Adjust your tie, suit up, and get ready to take action.

STAGE #1: INTRODUCTION TO CHAOS

Have you got what it takes to sell?

CHAPTER 1

Capital Reality and Base Reality: Your Safety Net

> *"This world we have created is a reflection of our society's collective ego and we are not our ego, we are the consciousness that listens to it speak."*
> *- Eckhart Tolle*

When we're born, nobody gives us the option to choose. There's simply no way to choose. Our parents didn't choose, neither did our grandparents, neither did their grandparents... Much less were we going to be able to.

But the important thing is that we are aware of the reality before embarking on our journey to becoming a true salesman.

There exist two worlds, two realities if you will.

The one we have created based on human volition, and the one that exists regardless of our volition.

One reality defines our greatest life objectives such as breathing, feeding ourselves, reproducing, and surviving. These are objectives that, regardless of our volition, are necessary and are the most basic building blocks of our existence.

Example: I'm hungry? Then I eat! I'm tired? Then I sleep!

The other reality defines our objectives like making a million dollars before 30, driving a Bentley, having a six-pack, and paying for 25 course dinners (with wine) that cost $1,000 a person.

They are two interdependent ecosystems, and yet very different.

Starting today we will talk about the reality that human volition has created as **"Capital Reality"** and we will talk about the reality that is independent from our volition as **"Base Reality."**

So where am I going with all of this?

A salesman must understand and embrace the fact that *"Capital Reality"* is not the source of happiness.

Bummed? Yeah, sorry, your happiness doesn't rely on having 3 billion dollars, on the car you drive, nor on the size of your biceps. Your happiness relies on you, on your life perspective, and on your ability to assign value to the most basic building blocks of our existence.

Believing that driving a Bentley will make you eternally happy is delusional, and a sickness that salespeople ourselves have inflicted upon humankind!

As salespeople, we have programmed the world to think that *"Capital Reality"* is the only thing that matters. Though commercials, dramatic advertisements, testimonials, sponsors, trials, free products, promotions, and blah, blah, blah.

But as they say in the drug world:

"An excellent drug dealer never gets addicted to his product."

And that's exactly what you have to know how to do.

You have to know how to tell that your happiness does not rely on money. (Although it hurts in no way at all!)

A salesman that accepts this has everything in their favor! Accepting it gives you a safety net to fall into and to bounce right back!

Don't believe for a second that accepting this, or setting up this "safety net," diminishes a great salesperson's motivation.

Everything is at stake.

To be successful in both realities, in both worlds, you need money. To get money you need to know how to sell, and whoever knows how to sell, gets their way.

But wait, before you even think it, <u>I'm not crazy or a hippie, I'm everything but.</u>

I hate the hippie mentality, and I'm the first to admit that I love money. Money has given me tremendous gifts in life; the chance to having control, security, abundance, and the chance to help the world in my own way.

And learning the reality of these two worlds and embracing it has made me realize that if tomorrow I'm broke with 10 dollars to my name… Everything's will be ok, because I'll be ok.

And instead of scaring myself, stressing out, and falling into a cycle of self-hate, stress, and despair surrounded by drugs and prostitutes *Jordan Belfort* style *(The Wolf of Wall Street),* I know that the only thing that lies before me is an opportunity to prove to myself that I'm good at this.

So when you invest in Wall Street and lose your first million, turn back to this chapter, reread it, and remember that everything's ok. Keep on crying because, even then it's going to hurt.

That's the game.

RECAP:

- "Capital Reality" is linked to human volition, "Base Reality" doesn't care if you want it or not, you need it to live!

- If great drug dealers don't get addicted to their product, great salespeople shouldn't either.

- Happiness is a product of your perspective and of the way you assign value to the different aspects of your life. It isn't a product of your bank account looking like a telephone number (Though that doesn't hurt anybody!).

- <u>Set up your safety net and prepare yourself because everything is at stake. Sell away!</u>

ACTION:

- Determine the cost of your Base Reality.

Use the format from the GOODIES section or draw two columns on a piece of paper and label one "CONCEPT" and the other one "MONEY."

After that, list everything you need to survive under "CONEPT." Not to have a luxurious lifestyle, not to be laying down on the beach in Cancun, not to go to the movie theater every weekend. Just write the basics for your living: rent (mortgage), electricity, water, gas, food, transportation, education, clothes (basic clothes, not Hugo Boss).

The purpose of this exercise is to identify your minimum viable income, to know how much is the minimum you need to earn each month so your "Base Reality" is not in jeopardy.

GOODIES:

- Download your Base Reality and Capital Reality here:
  http://www.workingwithcris.com/calculator/

Note: Don't determine your "Capital Reality" just yet, we'll do that in chapter 5 after having filtered and pinpointed your true definition of success.

CHAPTER 2

Your Relationship with Money

> *"I don't know how or why, but money always seems to make its way to me."*
> *-A salesperson in the first salesroom I worked in, unknown name*

Now that you know that your happiness should be completely separate from your desire to be richer than Warren Buffett, you must determine your mindset on money.

Somehow, you ended up as an adult and over the years your mind grew up collecting information from your surroundings. Picking up on attitudes, comments, actions, facts, and situations that happened around you. Experiences that you had no way of knowing if they were true, false, positive, or destructive. For you, they were simply *"normal."*

You gathered up lessons in your head about everything that surrounded you until creating a life vision. You adopted beliefs and opinions of the world based on information that well could be wrong. All of these opinions became your personality and your way of interacting with the planet.

And now, let's talk about money.

Your first impression of money probably was when you were little and you saw one of your friends go on vacation with their family all the time. They always had the newest toys and the most money to spend during lunch hour. And afterwards, you saw your other classmate who rode to school in an old, rusty car and who wore used school uniforms.

You knew that something was different but you didn't know exactly what. You were unaware of money's importance in human survival.
If, when speaking of money at home, your experiences and situations casted money in a light of conflict, scarcity, and negativity, it's possible you harbored jealous, angry, or resentful feelings towards your classmate. On the other hand, if money was an open, positive, and abundant topic at home, your feelings were probably of equality and affinity.

And here's the most important point:

When you were little you had no way of questioning the information you adopted and the effects they had on you, but today you do.

Today, in this exact moment, you have the possibility to analyze your relationship with money once and for all.

To give you a clear example of the difference between mindsets, here are a few typical phrases that we tend to hear from both sides of this dilemma.

It's important that, as you read the phrases, you start thinking about which side of the situation you're on. How good is my relationship with money?

Things that people who have a negative relationship with money say:

"It's hard..."
"If it just...."
"There's nothing I can do!"
"I've never been good with numbers."
"Money is the root of problems and greed."
"The rich are the problem of this country."
"Those things are not for people like us."
"Why do you want more? You have enough."

Things that people who have a positive relationship with money say:

"Let's find the solution."
"This is a great opportunity."
"Here, I'll lend you money."
"There's much more where this came from."
"Money always makes its way to me."
"I'm good with numbers and at producing money."
"Money is there, we just have to work for it."
"My life depends on me, and on no one else."
"Let's make it happen!"

There are billionaires that have obtained success thanks to the fact that they once had a terrible relationship with money; people that, due to their lack of money during childhood, employed that resentment to motivate themselves to work day and night until reaching their goals.

It's important that you know what your perspective on money is, and that you acknowledge it and that, starting today, you make the effort to shift these paradigms that have limited you in the past.

Scold yourself every time you find yourself speaking in negative terms!

RECAP:

- The quality of my relationship with money is directly proportional to how much I have, how fast it I get it, and how much of it I accumulate.

- The first step to improving my relationship with money is determining its current state.

- Having a bad relationship with money in the past has made billionaires – You could be one!

ACTION:

- Determine the quality of your relationship with money.

If you still are doubting the state of your relationship with money, answer the following questions:

1) How do you feel when you spend money? Remorseful? Happy? Guilty?

_____
_____
_____
_____

2) Which purchases do you try to save money on? Why?

_____
_____
_____
_____

3) Which purchases do you not care about spending a lot on? Why?

_____
_____
_____

4) Describe your current relationship with money:

_____
_____
_____

CHAPTER 3

The Sacred Trinity of "Get Rich"

"Faith without action is the worst strategy."
-Unknown

Do you truly believe that saving on that *Venti Latte Frappuccino* from Starbucks will make you richer?

I seriously doubt it.

But you have surely heard personal finance gurus shout at you:

"That coffee is 7 dollars today! But a cup of coffee per week for 50 years is $18,200 dollars!"

Frankly, I prefer to get the coffee.

$18,200 dollars in 50 years won't make me any richer. It won't get me out of serious health problems. It won't help me buy my mom her dream home. 18,200 dollars in 50 years won't give me the live that I deserve!

You know what really can give me the life I deserve?

Excellent conversation, closing another good business deal…. *While drinking a cup of coffee.*

Going on a date, getting to know the woman or man of my life… *While drinking a cup of coffee.*

A mindset of abundance that allows me to know that I am already producing more money even if I'm sitting down…. *While drinking a cup of coffee.*

Don't get me wrong, saving is extremely important. However, the amount of energy that people invest in saving, compared to the energy invested in producing, is ridiculously off-balance.

Saving isn't hard. Actually, the rules to keeping your personal finances in order and avoiding disasters are so simple there are just 5.

In order to keep learning how to sell, you have to swear to me that you will read these 5 rules and that you will hold them close to heart. I don't want you to be like *Vanilla Ice* and make millions selling just to lose them in a few years' time.

Basic Rules for Personal Finance

1) Spend less than you make (DUH!)
2) Have a 3-month-survival security fund.
3) Save constantly 10% to 30% of what you earn.
4) Have extensive health insurance coverage.
5) Learn to invest.

But do you know what your *"problem"* is with these five very basic rules?

Discipline

Saving requires discipline. And a great amount of self-control when facing the sickness of thinking that our *"Capital Reality"* will make us happy! Remember that we (the salespeople) have invented consumerism, and therefore we must be aware of its collateral effects and not fall for them.

Sadly, we live in a society where discipline is extremely scarce. People have ADD, Attention Deficit Disorder, and pay little attention to the world and their actions. This largely is a collateral effect of the consumerism that we have created.

Imagine this: According to studies from Yankelvich researchers, an average person is bombarded daily by 3,000 advertising stimuli… minimum! This number can grow to 20,000 depending on where you live.

There's your explanation for why you forget about saving when you see that new pair of shoes or the newest iPhone in the market. But this is no excuse! You need to be disciplined and get this together before learning to sell.

It's important that you know that there are 3 topics you need to master before having a lot of money, keeping it, and continually making it grow.

1) You need to know how to produce money (<u>SELLING</u>).
2) You need to know how to manage money (<u>SAVING</u>).
3) You need to know how to get money to work for you (<u>INVESTING</u>).

In this book we'll focus on the first point. **We'll learn to produce money by selling**.

Assuming that starting today you are going to be disciplined and handle your personal finances based on the five points explained above, we can move on to the most important topic: **SELLING!**

RECAP:

- If you want to make money, SELL! If you want to accumulate money, SAVE! If you want to multiply your money, INVEST!

- Don't waste energy saving cents. Focus your energy on selling more and on producing more money.
- The key to healthy personal finance is discipline (And to never stop producing).

- Personal finances in a nutshell; Spend less than you make, have a 3-month emergency fund, save 10%-30% of what you earn, have an extensive medical insurance policy.

ACTION:

- Determine the amount you must have in your emergency fund using the following formula:

Your "Base Reality" cost x 3 = Your Emergency Fund

- Budget for extensive medical insurance coverage.

Believe me, nothing shouts "BANKRUPTCY" louder than a medical emergency that you aren't ready for. There are good-quality plans for you and your family.

- Learn to invest.

Try it out and take it for a test drive, even if with small quantities. Start little by little and learn the investment game so that when the day comes and you have massive amounts of money, your decisions will be much more successful.

GOODIES:

- My article, "*7 Ways to Learn to Invest without Losing your Underwear in the Effort*" will give you the basis to be able to enter into the investment world.

Read it here:
http://workingwitheris.com/7waystolearntoinvestwithoutlosingyourunderwearintheeffort

CHAPTER 4

Salespeople Make the World Go Round

"Everything you want in life is a commission."
-Grant Cardone

It's true, salespeople make the world go round. But the reason why we do it is much less egotistical than the quote sounds.

We are not some elite group of salespeople, but in fact:

"Everybody in this world is a salesman."

Not one person exists on the face of the earth that doesn't need to sell something. An idea, a product, or themselves. We all have something to sell and in every communication process someone is selling something and the other person is buying it.

Selling is a requirement to live. Whoever doesn't sell, spends their whole life buying! And we are not talking about impulsive shopping at Rolex or Cartier. We're talking about how there are people who indiscriminately buy ideas, opinions, dreams, and goals that aren't theirs!

There are people that, for not accepting their role as a salesperson, surrender this power to others and allow others to sell them dreams and convictions that aren't their own. Ones often that are not even positive for them.

<u>Imagine that! There are people that work for 50 years building up somebody else's dream!</u>

This is why we must come out of the salesman closet and take control over this ship that is our life.

Everybody sells! Do you want proof?

You're a freelancer? You sell yourself as a product or service
You're an office worker? You sell yourself to your boss for a raise or promotion.
You're an entrepreneur? You sell yourself to investors as the best alternative.
You're a boyfriend/girlfriend? You sell yourself daily to your significant other as the best option.
You're a student? You sell yourself to your professor as the most intelligent student.
You're a human being? You sell your image and personality to the world.

When you embrace your identity as a salesman and invest time and money into developing that side of your life, your chances of getting what you want increase by 300%.

Remember that everything in life is just a sale away, and everything that you want in this life is a commission.

Do you want a million dollars?

You need to sell 100 products worth $10,000 dollars or 1,000 products worth $1,000 dollars.

Do you want to get the woman of your dreams?

You need to sell her the idea that you are the man of her dreams.

Do you want to teach your kids?

You need to speak to them in their language and sell them the lessons you want them to learn.

Do you want to eat at an Argentinian restaurant and your wife wants sushi?

You need to know how to sell your opinion!

Survival of the fittest started out by knowing how to sell.

And even if it's illogical… people tend to run from sales instead of embracing them as the greatest power they possess: the only way that they have of influencing their daily life.

Why? Because they have tried and failed.

Or worse, because they fell for some terrible timeshare pitch or multi-level marketing scheme that left them scarred for life.

One way or another, the fact that there are not many people that dare to dive headfirst into the life of a salesman is excellent news for us.

Less competition, less well-trained people, and many more opportunities to take advantage of.

Everybody in this world is a salesman.

Accept it, embrace it, and….

Get ready.

RECAP:

- Everybody, absolutely everybody in this world, is a salesman!

- If you don't sell, you're buying the ideas, dreams, and goals of others!

- Embrace your role as a salesman and get your way!

- Everything in this life is just a sale away, and everything you want is the commission that you're after.

ACTION:

- Get up! Get motivated! Love what you do and your profession!

Right now, this instant, I want you to type up on the computer a list of the 5 best things that knowing how to sell has given you. They could be the best 5 sales of your life, the world vision that selling has given you, or whatever you think fit.

I want you to write it down right now and post it to Facebook, Twitter, or whichever social network!

I want you to embrace your role as a salesman, to make it public, and to teach the world what you are capable of!

Example:

"These are the 5 Reasons why I LOVE sales:

1) They give me the power to know that I own my life!

2) They allow me to sell myself to my significant other and love them every day!

3) They have taught me that there are people that get things DONE or people that make EXCUSES, but there is no combination thereof.

4) They've given me the pleasure of driving a Porsche Carrera! ☺

5) They keep me from being dependent on ANYBODY!

#EverybodySells

Don't forget to tag me so I can see it and use the hashtag #EverybodySells so that EVERYBODY can see the amount of energy and commitment that TODAY you have with your personal success. And if you don't have me on social networks yet, you're losing some incredible content. Add me today!

Facebook: www.facebook.com/crisurzua
Twitter: www.twitter.com/crisurzua
LinkedIn: www.linkedin.com/in/crisurzua

CHAPTER 5

Your Personal Definition of Success

"Listen to your own voice, listen to your own soul. Too many people live to listen to the noise of the world."
- Unknown

Note: Every single one of this chapter's exercises can potentially change your life. If you do them, I assure you that you will have foundation to be the #1 salesman in history. If you don't do them, I can't assure of you anything. Read carefully.

Oh success. Sweet, sweet success.

For many people, you're something only encountered on TV. Or when they read online about Hollywood's #1 star, or about the latest 20-year-old internet millionaire. For others, success is not just the destination, it's the journey; it's a way of life.

The difference between these two groups is that the second group realized the importance of investing the necessary time into finding and creating their definition of success. By doing this, they didn't "buy" somebody else's definition of success.

Going about life without this definition is simply filling up your existence over and over again with meaningless tasks, meaningless sales, and even meaningless relationships, throughout your entire life.

So, why is it so important to take the time to make your own definition? Because without it, you're wasting the most valuable non-renewable resource you have: Your time!

Time is the most valuable non-renewable resource that we have!

Take this concept and treasure it for the rest of your life.

Everything you postpone, everything you say "stops" you from reaching your definition of success, every emotional problem that you drag with you: these are all factors that make you weak and less agile in your decision-making skills. And when we can't make agile decisions, we waste massive amounts of time.

You want to know how to make agile decisions?

You have to know where you're going; you have to know what your definition of success is.

I have the hope that you are already questioning what your own definition of success is, but before you start driving 120 miles per hour inside this labyrinth of questions and answers that we all have in our head, you need to know that there exists no universal concept of success.

Success means something different for each one of us. It's directly related to your values, your ethics, your history, and the way in which every one of these factors are set as priorities in your life.

There are many cases (and you may be one of them) where even in a successful position, the person feels incomplete. You may be a successful vice-president, a CEO of your own company, an important executive, or even a celebrity, and even then you don't feel completely satisfied with your career or even with your life.

Why does this happen? Because you haven't taken steps towards your definition of success.

Often, the hardest thing to do is to distance yourself from something that may be amazing for someone, but not good enough for you.

So, how do I make my own definition of success to stop wasting time?

First of all, you have to understand the following 5 Basic Principles for Success. They will help you to have a better perspective of this quite elusive term –

> ✓ **This is step #1 on your path to defining success.**

Basic Principle for Success #1: Success is holistic.

> Your definition for success must include every aspect of your life: work, health, love, life purpose, spiritual beliefs – Everything! It must be the goal and the path you follow throughout your life to achieve wellbeing in every aspect. If you are successful in the professional world, but not in your health, your vision of success is incomplete.

Basic Principle for Success #2: Success motivates!

> Your definition for success must give you the energy, drive, and emotion necessary to chase after it! You have to feel the vibrations of this energy all the way to your core when talking about it. If you don't feel it, or the feeling quickly evaporates away leaving you with no specific results, you haven't found your true definition – Keep looking, don't settle.

Basic Principle for Success #3: Success give you happiness.

> It's inevitable. Once you've found your definition, you will feel your soul lift, as if granting you an understanding that

you have found it at last. You'll recognize with a smile the exact moment it happens. Be careful with what makes you money, but doesn't make you happy. Eliminate those comfort zones!

Basic Principle for Success #4: Success is dynamic.

> Just like everything in life, your definition of success isn't necessarily the same today as it will be when you are 80 years old. Acknowledge this and make the proper decisions that allow you to be flexible enough to change over time.

Read over these concepts again.

You'll go back to them once you have written down your definition for the first time. These *Basic Principles for Success* will be your guide from now on. Whenever you wish to check if your definition is still exact and you wish to keep to your priorities, return to this list.

And if you've noticed, good for you. I said five points and I only gave you four… We'll talk about the fifth at a later point.

✓ **Step #2 in your path for defining success:**

The path to discovering our definition of success continues by determining the priorities that govern your life. Every minute that we live, we are forced to make decisions. Every decision that we've made, determines the present that we live in.

Have you ever made a decision only to realize afterwards that you really didn't want the choice you made?

This normally happens when we are distracted or when we are unaware of our priorities. There are people who have blown out the candles of their 89th birthday without knowing what it is that they really value, or who don't understand how their life brought them to where they are.

Our priorities in life are directly related to the decisions we make day to day.

ACTION:

I want you to grab a piece of paper, or if you are a little more tech-oriented to open up your computer, and to write down **in no particular order** the most valuable 15 or 20 things in your life. The things that you have the strongest emotional connection with; the things that make you happy. They can be people (family, friends, partners, coworkers…), values (honesty, integrity, dignity…), feelings (feeling accomplished, happiness, love…), attitudes (professionalism, integrity, being social…), goals (starting your own business, writing a book, etc…), even your job, your car, etc.

Anything that you're passionate about!

Write down anything you feel currently affects your decision-making process. I'll do this exercise with you, too, to give you a better example.

CRIS'S PRIORITIES

My little brother	Money	Family
Romantic Love	Recognition	Feeling accomplished

Being super motivated	Being healthy	Writing and Reading
Life design	Selling	Psychology
Music	Traveling	Socializing

Once you've written the most important 15 or 20 things in your life, list them according to their priority! Make a list starting with the most meaningful thing for you right now, and end with what you believe is least relevant in your life. This can be a tricky process – I'll ask you take your time and be very objective with yourself.

Note: This list is private and for your eyes only. No one other than you should have any opinion or advice regarding this list. Actually, they shouldn't even see it.

So forget about if Aunt Mary will notice that you think your dog is more valuable than her. And please don't overthink your decisions.

I'll also do this exercise with you.

MY PRIORITIES IN ORDER OF IMPORTANCE

1) My little brother
2) Being healthy
3) Being super motivated
4) Money

5) Feeling personally accomplished
6) Romantic Love
7) Family
8) Recognition
9) Socialization
10) Selling
11) Traveling
12) Reading and writing
13) Music
14) Life-style design
15) Psychology

There you go. That's my list of priorities at this moment.

The funny part of this exercise is to not overcomplicate. What you really want to do is pay more attention to the big issues that jump out at you. Since this is what gives you the answers that help you to find that definition of success, and that also help you to make any decision in general. This last exercise is a great tool that you can reuse every time you have to make an important decision (check the GOODIES section at the end of the chapter to use the official format).

Example: Let's say tomorrow I receive an offer to move to Sweden for the next 3 years to implement a new promotion strategy for the Swedish government, and they offer me the equivalent of 5 million dollars per year to do it (*ring, ring,* Swedish Government).

Obviously, this would make me really happy because it suits my priority #5 (feeling personally accomplished), my #4 (money), #8 (recognition), #10 (selling) and many other priorities.

Nonetheless, I would have to ensure that my brother (priority #1) is safe and happy with my parents while I am away. I would have to do whatever necessary to stay healthy during the trip (priority #2), as well as having to evaluate which other of my priorities could be in conflict with this decision. Would I be willing to go even if my significant other decided to stay? Would this somehow get in the way with my family life?

I repeat, it's very important not to overcomplicate things. Pay attention to every issue as they come forth. Don't overanalyze small variables. This will only distract you from the main purpose of this exercise.

Step #3 (and last step) on your path to defining success: Make your own definition of success!

Up to this point, you've learned that we have varying personal opinions about what success means, and that finding your own definition will help you to pave the way, as well as the goals that you should aim for.

You've also learned some of the Basic Principles for Success that allow you to grasp this concept's nature on a deeper level. And you have identified your life priorities…

Now you are ready to determine what success means for you.

Take a piece of paper or open up your computer again and write down the following:

"(*YOUR NAME)*'S DEFINITION OF SUCCESS. DATE: XX/XX/XXXX"

My definition of success at this very moment is:"

Make sure to write down the date. It's of the upmost importance!

Once you've written that down, start writing and don't stop until your hand hurts. Make sure to write everything down you associate with success. Include everything that you have to do before you die or before your life feels incomplete. If you want your definition of success to be flexible and change over the years, write "how" you want to be instead of "what" you want to have.

Remember that there is no worse regret than regretting to not having done something. Don't be afraid of thinking big!! Think "Hollywood" size. Don't limit yourself. It doesn't matter how ridiculous it may sound.

Once you've finished writing your definition, read it several times. Correct it, add more, erase what doesn't make sense, and edit it until you feel proud of it, and of yourself.

You are now one of the few people in the world who are aware of what success means to them. And you are closer to reaching it than ever before.

I'll also do this exercise with you, of course. Here's my current definition of success.

CRIS'S DEFINITION OF SUCCESS 04/06/2013

My definition of success at this moment is... *Being a congruent and ethical man with my beliefs and their priorities. Never allowing anyone to limit my dreams, and always having the motivation and discipline necessary to reach them. I want to be a man who gives and loves with no expectations. To be a man who holds no resentment. I want to reach every one of my goals, be it financial, professional, physical, or spiritual. I want to be humble, service-oriented, and to never stop learning. I want every person that has contact with me to be benefited in some way. And I never want to lose the ability to enjoy my Base Reality.*

Now make sure to verify that your definition of success, the *5 Basic Principles for Success,* and your life priorities are congruent. Once you have, print them out. Make several copies and hang them up in places where you'll constantly see them: Next to your bed, on the refrigerator door, in your wallet, and in your office.

You did it! Now you know the goal that you are selling for. You no longer are selling to chase the idea that Brad Pitt and Angeline Jolie sold you. Starting today you will be selling with the singular goal of being true to yourself, your personality, and to your definition of success.

And for everybody that was waiting for it, here is the fifth, the last, and the most important of the *5 Basic Principles for Success*...

- **Basic Principle for Success #5:** Success is always obtainable.

I don't care if society tells you that you are too old or that you're a mess. It doesn't matter if you yourself feel that you've made world's worst decisions. Success doesn't place judgement and it never leaves us. It's us that leave it. In order to reach success you need courage, discipline, strength, and, most importantly, you need to stay hungry. You need to want it so badly that not one day goes by that you don't do something that brings you one step closer to it.

Commit to your success. It's there, waiting for you.

RECAP:

- Analyze your definition of success! Did you define it? Or did you buy it from someone else?

- Time is your most valuable non-renewable resource, not money.

- Do you understand how success works? The 5 Basic Principles for Success are key to understanding and defining our much sought-after friend.

- Your life priorities are directly related to how you make decisions day to day. What are your priorities?

What is your definition of success?

ACTION:

Other than the incredible action you have already taken in this chapter, it's time to do something else for you, and for your success as a salesman.

- Determine the cost of your Capital Reality.

Now's the time to dream. In the same two columns, or even better, in the format that you'll find in the GOODIES section, find out how much it would cost to live your ideal life, your "Capital Reality."

Now is the time for you to include and to estimate the cost for everything you would love to have. A personal driver, two cleaning ladies at home, the best education for your family, your monthly mortgage, food every day, a monthly budget for fun and going out, a monthly budget for vacationing, etc. Include everything that you've ever dreamed of as a requirement to counting yourself as successful!

Keep this number handy to make use of it at a later point.

GOODIES:

- Download your Base Reality and Capital Reality calculator here: http://www.workingwithcris.com/calculator

- Download the Guide to designing your personal definition of success here:
  http://www.workingwithcris.com/guidetodesigningyourpersonaldefinitionofsuccess

CHAPTER 6

The Pianist (The Bad Reputation of Sales)

> *"Relativity applies to physics, not ethics."*
> *- Albert Einstein*

How many people have you met that are ashamed to work in sales?

There are even jokes about it!

I was raised by two of the best timeshare salesmen I have ever met. Sales payed for my education, food, and the roof over my head ever since the day I was born. This is why I have so much faith in the industry.

I remember a joke my dad used to tell:

It was career day at Billy's school, and every student had to stand up next to the board and tell their classmates what their parents did for a living. Parents had also been invited to the class and were at the back of the classroom.

Susan goes first:

"Well, my dad is a doctor. He specializes in heart diseases and he saves lives for a living!"

Everyone applauds.

Then Jimmy goes:

"My dad is a firefighter. He wakes up really early every day to be ready for any emergency and save people's lives!"

Bravo! Everybody applauds.

Suddenly, it's Billy's turn to stand up at the front.

"Well, my dad is a pianist in a brothel."

An awkward silence washes over the entire room and Billy quickly exits the front of the class.

After the class, Billy's dad asks him furiously:

"Billy! Why in the world did you say that!?"

Billy answers:

"Come on dad.... What did you want me to tell them? That you sell timeshares?"

Da dum tssssss…..

End of joke.

Hearing that joke makes me want to laugh and cry at the same time, but it's an excellent reality check.

Unfortunately, sales have a bad rep, and for several reasons.

Here's a list:

- Unscrupulous, lying salesmen (who should be thrown in jail).
- Bad salesmen that use high-pressure techniques.
- Companies that burn 9 prospects to sell to 1 through high-pressure techniques (unsustainable techniques).

- Personal failures in sales, meaning people that have tried, had no decent training, and failed for obvious reasons.
- The typical friend that invites you out and ends up wanting to sell a multilevel marketing scheme to you (very bad prospecting).

What more do you want?

With all these reasons, it's more than enough to hate an entire industry!

If we weren't all salesmen, if sales weren't what keeps our society going, they would have already shut us down.

What's interesting is the reaction that the world has had regarding sale's bad reputation. This is a phenomenon that I call "camouflage."

"Camouflage" is simply an illogical way that every industry on the planet has decided to subtly "hide" their salespeople.

If you hadn't realized, there no longer exists salesman as a job title!

Now every company has:

- Representatives
- Account Executive
- Coordinators
- Advisors
- Concierge
- Assistants
- Managers
- Brand Ambassadors
- Analysts

Any job title is better than simply titling someone "Salesman."

The term salesman has been demoted to the sock drawer in an attempt to "camouflage" the true intention we all have, which (even with the nice and fancy job title) is still to sell.

This attempt at camouflaging is useful and has worked. Why? Because people are illogical! Do you think that people don't know they are salesmen? Of course they do! Do you think that people don't know that you will earn a commission if they accept your subtle "recommendation?" Come on! Don't insult us by saying no!

Your customer is highly educated! They already read on TripAdvisor that the hotel concierge is the salesman. They already spoke to their friends to ask about your reputation as an "advisor." Your customer will get defensive even if you have some kind of trendy and fancy title!

The two main goals behind making you aware of this are:

1) That you understand the only response to, "Are you going to sell me something?" is "Of course! But I'm not going to sell you something you aren't entirely in love with" and…

2) That you accept and embrace your need to learn to sell. And to stop giving a bad name to our industry.

We'll talk much more about ethics in the next chapter, but as I said at the beginning, this is not a book for you if you think that when selling, lying is necessary.

Selling is necessary, turning up the contrast in photos is necessary, creating emotions is necessary; but lying is never necessary!

So decide now if what you're going to be is an amateur salesman that soils the prestige of the industry, or if you're going to be a star salesman who inspires the world. This is your last chance to stop wasting time reading this book.

Remember what I told you at the beginning: "This book is not for people who think that lying is part of the sales process." If you throw this book out the window, I won't judge you, don't worry.

<u>Being ethical is your decision, and yours alone</u>

RECAP:

- It is my mission as a salesperson to be the example, and not part of the group that has given a bad reputation to the industry.

- "Camouflage" in sales: The illogical title that works.

- Are you going to be a salesman who values the ethic… or just pathetic?

ACTION:

- Make a statement!

Right now, at this moment, decide that, no matter how tempting it is in our industry, you will be an ethical salesperson, who never would hurt nor cheat a customer. Make the commitment.

Open up your Twitter, Facebook, or favorite social network and post this:

"An outstanding salesman NEVER needs to lie! #EverybodySells"

Let the world know what type of salesman you are, make the commitment, say it out loud and sell yourself to the world as an ethical and professional salesman.

Not as an amateur.

CHAPTER 7

Less Hawaiian Shirts, More Well-Tailored Suits

"You can't have a million dollar dream, with a minimum wage work ethic."
- Zig Ziglar

Hey!

That's great you're still reading. That means you've decided to be a salesperson who inspires others and not a scumbag of a salesman that continually contributes to the bad rep caused by a few.

Now that's out of the way, I have to show you why you need to be less like a *Hawaiian Shirt* and more like a *Well-Tailored Suit*.

The *Hawaiian Shirt*; the official uniform of the 80's/90's shark/timeshare salesman. Comfortable, baggy, one-size-fits-all, cool, and synonymous with zero commitment and relaxation.

Great!

Now, get away from me. I don't want to do business with you.

This famous shirt, in my mind, is the symbol of everything that's wrong in the industry. Why? Because it's fiercely ugly, a symbol of conformity, and because I would never hand over $40,000 dollars of my money to somebody wearing one.

"But, Cris, we're selling vacations, we have to inspire relaxation."

Then inspire relaxation through pictures, videos, and a walk on the beach! But don't expect me to be comfortable handing over my precious money to a *Hawaiian Shirt*.

Now, why should we be more like a *Well-Tailored Suit?*

Being a well-tailored suit isn't about your dress code (we'll dive into that later), it's about your attitude towards sales.

Whoever's a *Well-Tailored Suit* is able to inspire confidence, credibility, and success in all of their customers, regardless of size.

Whoever's a *Well-Tailored Suit* is a sales professional, not an amateur.

Whoever's a *Well-Tailored Suit* attributes the necessary seriousness to their profession, invests in their own growth, and sees sales as a way of life, not as a temporary job. They see sales as a career, not a chore.

Being a *Well-Tailored Suit* is about your priorities.

If your priority is making an eternally happy customer, improving their life with your product, and in the process making a huge commission and improving your own… You're a well-tailored suit.

If your priority is making a huge commission with a bad product and an even worse sale, you're a *Hawaiian Shirt*.

A *Well-Tailored Suit* doesn't look for shortcuts sacrificing quality.

<u>Ask yourself:</u>

What type of suit are you? What type of fiber are you made of? How much investment is there in your suit? Are you worth buying? Is it worth buying with you?

So… **Suit up!**

And sell away.

RECAP:

- Are you a Hawaiian Shirt or a Well-Tailored Suit?

ACTION:

- Please throw out your Hawaiian Shirt.

CHAPTER 8

The 5 Hawaiian Shirt Mistakes

"Big egos have little ears"
- Robert Schuller

Hawaiian Shirts, also known as amateur or mediocre salesmen, aren't bad just for using the shirt. They're bad for an endless number of reasons. The shirt is just a byproduct.

To make sure Hawaiian Shirts don't magically appear in your closet, I beg you to never make these mistakes.

Mistake #1: They talk too much

Contrary to what people think, selling is more about knowing how to listen than knowing how to talk.

We all know how to talk! It's not rocket science! And on top of that, human beings are conditioned into believing that we're masters of ultimate truth, when in reality, we're not.

Don't talk too much. Work on carefully listening and understanding your customer. Learn to ask the right questions and construct phrases that activate your prospect's emotions.

Remember that nothing you learn today will come from your own mouth. In the same way, if you want to grow and learn, close your mouth and open your mind.

Mistake #2: They see truth as a disadvantage

Your product can't do something? Say it before it becomes a disadvantage! Get rid of that objection before it even comes up. That house you want to sell has humidity problems? First mention it yourself and show your customer exactly why this house would be a good investment.

You sell timeshare? Don't say it's timeshare. Say that it's the BEST timeshare ever and that not knowing that is to lose money and quality in every single trip.

Hawaiian Shirts are terrified by the truth, because they're too lazy to anticipate the objections your product has by nature.

Your customer will always know how to see through your lies and if they don't notice from the beginning, sooner or later they will come around to bite you in the butt.

There is nothing more powerful than the truth.

Mistake #3: They don't believe in their product

How do you dare sell me something that you don't even believe in?

If you wouldn't buy the product you're offering, don't you dare sell it. Believing in your product will not only give you the necessary credibility for the sale, but it will also give you the level of energy and passion to advocate for opportunities, services, and products that truly add value to your customers' life.

Look at true salesmen, at *Well-Tailored Suits*. Generally, they own or use the products that they promote so much.

Mistake #4: They assume

This is the most common mistake of the *Hawaiian Shirts*. They assume, skip steps, and later ask themselves, "Why didn't I make the sale?"

Assume NOTHING! And hold no prejudice against ANYONE!

You think your customer isn't interested? Are those your hundreds of years of experience in body language talking? WRONG! Assume nothing. There are people who have a resting facial expression of indifference.

You think your customer doesn't have the funds to purchase your product? WRONG! Never assume this. Your definition of how a wealthy person should look may be very far off.

Instead of defaulting to assumptions and prejudice, ask, socialize, and get to know your customer before starting the sale. Always try personalizing your service and your relationship instead of making assumptions and looking for shortcuts.

Mistake #5: They stress out

Why do they stress out? Because they don't follow the basic rules of personal finance that we visited in chapter 3, and because they believe that their "Capital Reality" is the source of all happiness.

You've already set up a safety net. Take the leap, and don't stress out.

RECAP:

- An outstanding salesman, one wearing a *Well-Tailored Suit* and not a *Hawaiian Shirt*, listens more and speaks less.

- The truth is never a disadvantage.

- Selling something you don't believe in or that you wouldn't buy is a class of lying.

- An outstanding salesman assumes NOTHING and inquires about EVERYTHING!

- Build a mental "safety net" and don't stress out!

ACTION:

- Have you thrown out your Hawaiian shirts yet?

    (Hmmmm... Just checking)

CHAPTER 9

The Future of Sales

"The future started yesterday, and we're already late"
- John Legend

"Hello Robert, we have to ask you to pack up your things and to retire. You no longer work for the company."

"What?! But why?!"

"We now have an iPhone app that does everything you do for free and that isn't so terribly bad-tempered. Thanks. You can pack up now."

No, don't worry. You won't be replaced by an iPhone app.

Well, at least if you're a *Well-Tailored Suit*. If you're a *Hawaiian Shirt* I can't promise you a thing.

Many people have asked me about what I think to be the future of sales in 10, 20, or 50 years. People want control and security. It's normal for us to want see where we stand and where to work towards before the rest to gain an edge.

This is my two cents:

I completely agree with Peter Thiel, founder of Paypal, when he states that technology will not replace humans, and much less salesmen.

Today's technology has an incredible power to quickly and efficiently process billions of bits of information. This process allows us to get to know our customers better, to see patterns, measure our efforts, and fine tune our strategies.

Machines are great at analyzing massive amounts of information, humans beings are not.

But there does exist something that machines have yet to be as good as humans at, and that is…. *in being human.*

In knowing how consider non-quantified information in the decision-making process, in knowing how to navigate a social context, and in understanding the emotions that cause humans to act so illogically.

But what happens when machines and their information processing are coupled with an emotional and feeling human being?

The best results possible.

There are hundreds of stories about how the human-machine alliance has yielded better results than when each one works independently. We see it in credit card fraud detection: Machines detect patters, analysts confirm if there is or is not risk. We see it in market studies: Machines detect patterns, and marketers confirm if there is indeed real opportunity.

A human-machine alliance is the future.

In conclusion, you're not going to be replaced by a machine, but you are going to be working much more with them. I even would say that your efficacy as a salesman and your sales margin will be directly dependent on the quality of your relationship with technology.

I'm leaving you here 10 statements that, after my years of study, I would make. Only time will tell if they are true or not.

1) The quality of your relationship with technology will be directly proportional to your earnings as a salesman. The human-machine alliance will be of the upmost importance.

2) Social and negotiation skills will be more valuable than ever, but opportunities will be reduced to a certain number of subject specialists. Only *Well-Tailored Suits* will survive. There will no longer be space for *Hawaiian Shirts*.

3) There will not exist a professional salesman who is unaware of their metrics.

4) CRM software (Customer Relationship Management) will be essential to managing effective relationships with your customer.

5) It will be necessary to add 5 times more value to a product to be able to sell it.

6) Speed will be the name of the game. If you aren't up to date on the new trends in technology, your competition will eat you alive. As Bob Dylan says, *"He not busy being born, is busy dying."*

7) If you're no one online, you'll be nobody to your customers.

8) Customers will make 90% of the purchase before even meeting you. Your emotional touch only will be the cherry on the pie to close the deal.

9) Everything will be focused on customer service and customization.

10) Everyone will be an online brand, but few will truly be good in real life, and that will be the difference.

By keeping all these points in mind, you can have an idea of what direction you should take your career into as a salesperson, your business's commercial strategy, and your ventures.

Selling will always play a part of our lives. Bartering, exchanging, and influence will always be present. Though if you don't anticipate change and you don't embrace technology as an opportunity, your customers will ask you to pack your bags.

RECAP:

- Machines will not replace salesmen, but your earnings will be dependent on the quality of your relationship with technology.

- The future of sales is in the personalization of service.

- Speed will be the name of the game in sales and in business in general.

ACTION:

- Audit the quality of your relationship with technology.

Answer the following questions:

1) What technological features should I incorporate into my sales process?

_____
_____
_____
_____

2) What technology does the competition use that I don't?

_____
_____
_____
_____

3) What futuristic initiatives can I apply to my business to sell more, offer better service, and to win over my customers even more? (Do a little research for this question, dream, and look for the means to make them reality).

_____
_____
_____
_____

The goal of this audit is for you to discover innovative opportunities in order to sell more and take your business to the next level.

At the same time, analyze if technology intimidates you or excites you. You need to make sure that as a salesperson, you see technology as a tool to success and not as an inconvenience or obstacle.

Don't settle! Keep growing!

GOODIES:

- Modernize!

I've got 5 apps for your cellphone that you need to get NOW! And even better, they're 100% free and user friendly, even for the most newbie tech-salesman.

Download them for free here:
http://www.workingwithcris.com/5appsforsalesmen

CHAPTER 10

6 Things you NEED to know before getting into SALES

> *"Salesmanship is limitless. Our very living is selling."*
> *-James Cash Penney*

If you're a follower of my blog, you probably recognize that header. This header changed my life in such a ridiculously random way, that I still can't believe.

One day, after many years of selling, I decided to leave my comfort zone and do something I always had wanted to do.

I decided to start a blog about sales.

A blog where I could share the maniacal, obsessive, funny, and random situations that happen in the life of a salesman. A blog that salespeople can relate to, laugh about, and know that they are not alone, and more importantly, that they were extremely intelligent to dedicate their lives to this profession.

I wrote my first article called "*6 things you NEED to know before getting into SALES,*" I posted it on the blog (with spelling mistakes to the horror of more than one grammar Nazi out there), I shared it to Facebook and I went to bed.

36 hours later, I checked Facebook and the blog and….. Holy cow!

40,000 hits, more than 500 shares, hundreds of comments on the blog and hundreds of people trying to contact me to share stories and laugh for a bit.

After those 36 hours, weeks followed where the article flooded the internet like Hurricane Wilma in Cancun in 2005 (I'm from Cancun and I'm a survivor. I have the right to make light of it). Lots of invitations to teach courses, conferences, and training. So much positive energy and most importantly: <u>Attention for an ignored community.</u>

The community of salespeople had been ignored for years, working under the *"Camouflage"* and feeling underappreciated. The blog opened doors for the topic and gave us all a laugh.

You have no idea how much I appreciate your continued support since those first 36 hours up to today. I love you all.

Without further ado, here are the *6 Things you NEED to know before getting into SALES* – This is your last opportunity to run.

'6 Things you NEED to know before getting into SALES by Cris Urzua.'

If someone had warned me of these 6 points 7 years ago, I probably still would have gotten into the world of sales…

BUT!

I would have been much more prepared for the whirlwind of information, emotion, up and downs, and situations – BORDERLINE ridiculous – that a salesperson has to deal with every day.

It doesn't matter if you sell real estate, timeshares, diamonds, Mennonite cheese, or lettuce (...I've got a good friend that made millions selling lettuce), this list will make you laugh, scare those who think sales are "easy money," and motivate those who are truly interested in getting into the industry.

Let's get started!

#1: Commissions: Your new best friend
Forget about waiting around, watching for the clock to strike 5 to rush home. And say goodbye to those "twenty minute" Lunch Breaks where you take an hour and a half cutting off the ends of your sandwich into your favorite geometric figure from grade school.

If you want to be successful in this industry, you have to be on your game, ready to serve customers whenever they need it. Wasted time = missed sales and missed sales = credit score through the floor. The run-of-the-mill office worker mindset of "show up, do my time, and get out" doesn't work in this industry. YOU are the only one responsible for ensuring your time makes money for you. Commit or quit!

#2: Your Emotions to the Blender: You'll be REJECTED all day long

If you're not being told no, you're not selling enough. Handling rejection is one of the reasons jobs in sales are so well paid... Why? Because it's horrible! And it's normal and even good that this stirs up your emotions. At the end of the day they didn't say no to your product, they said no to you as a salesman. And if you assume that responsibility, you have the power to change your approach and improve your results.

Do you remember in grade school when Hannah said that she didn't want to be your girlfriend? Well, sales are going to put you in that situation several times a day, and sooner or later you're going to get a few yes's.

#3: Your Fellow Salesmen: Are crazy (And you are too)

Think about it. You're surrounded by passionate, emotional, and simply imaginative people. It doesn't matter what you sell, sales attract a variety of characters from A to Z. You'll see it ALL in the sales world: grumpy old men, junior millionaires, seductive bombshells, stupidly positive people, drugs, people who don't stop talking, and success stories in spite of impossible odds. Nothing I tell you will prepare you for your fellow salesmen!

And every once in a while, you'll find people who are outstanding human beings (depending heavily on what company you're working in and what product you're selling), and I guarantee that you'll have a good laugh with all of them (even the most imaginative) at least once.

#4 Spontaneous Anger: Customers who've gotten botox or something personal?

The moment will come where you simply don't click with a customer. Why? You don't know, neither do they, but they hate you as if you ate Golden Retriever puppies for breakfast. These cases are rare, but sooner or later it'll happen to you and it's interesting to see that even with your best smile, your best joke, your new cologne, that the customer doesn't fall under your charm.

What do I do? You have two options: Change of face (meaning let someone else serve the customer) or stop judging the poor grumpy guy and get on with the sale. Often, it's you who has the attitude problem and not the customer. Or maybe the customer has just received terrible news and it's nothing personal. In any of these cases never stop asking, "How would you like to pay, sir?"

#5 Law of the Doughnut Hole: Do you see the hole before the doughnut?

Unfortunately, our profession is plagued by negative people who are used to living in their mediocre zone that provide them with "enough" to get by every day. However, if your goal is to be the best, the #1, the Jordan Belfort (but ethical and healthy, we hope) of your sales team...

You can't allow yourself to be negative!

Stay away from anyone who's negative around you. Get used to seeing things from a positive angle. Speak in terms of abundance and not scarcity. Have downtime. Be proactive. And when you catch yourself buying some excuse or negative thought – Spit it out! You can't allow yourself to lose time wandering and lowering your energy level.

#6 The First Paycheck

No, I'm not "literally" talking about your first paycheck.

I'm talking about that first paycheck, the first one that you got and saw the amount and said, "HELLLL YEEESSSS! THIS IS WHY I WORK IN SALES!" That paycheck where you started to think, "My office worker friends make this in a month, and I made it in one sale." That check will be your new PR (Personal Record) and it will be your reference point for any other check to come. That check that will let you take your significant other to the city's best restaurant to celebrate.

When the check comes, there's no turning back.

You're a salesman, and you're in it for life.

Whether you like it or not, sales are a requirement to being successful in life since #EverybodySells. And if you aren't selling, you're buying somebody else's idea and vision. The sooner you adopt the salesman's mentality, you study up, and you practice up, the greater the probabilities that you'll be successful.

#EverybodySells

RECAP:

- Success is dependent upon your bravery to take action, not on time. Success can be immediate, you just need to be brave to make things happen.

- The power of the internet is legendary. Use it to sell your product.

- I love you all, truly, I love you. Thank you.

ACTION:

- Do something that scares you.

What have you been putting off out of fear? Or why is it not the right time? Or because of "what they'll say?"

Determine TODAY what you've been putting off and make a conscious decision to make it happen.

Your success and how fast you get it is dependent on no one other than you.

CHAPTER 11

The Manifest

"Thinking too much usually is a product of doing too little."
-Yehuda Berg

What's a manifest? Easy! It's a public declaration of principles and intentions.

And this is the Manifest of Sales. This is the Manifest of the Salesman. This is the Manifest of the *Well-Tailored Suits*.

Print it out and read it every day, post it on Facebook with the hashtag #EverybodySells and revisit it every time you have doubts about who you are and why you sell.

Use it to stay motivated!

Life is a sale and getting my way is dependent on no one else other than myself. Everything that I want is a sale away: goals, fame, success; everything a sale away, an attempt, <u>a step above average.</u>

Be terrified of mediocrity. I sell ethically, I sell as I would want to be sold to. I know the lies but I don't need to use them; I know the way out but I NEVER plan on using it.

I am deaf to all criticism, all negativity. I build my own environment. I am an ecosystem beyond the power of your words. I hold zero excuses. I am the sole source of my motivation. Providing, growing, learning, or dying. Always one step ahead.

I keep my priorities clear, and I don't believe in coincidences. Luck is an illusion for people that fail to recognize my hard work and all my preparation. I believe in life. I believe in my definition of success. I believe in the way I want to live, in the way I want to help. I take control, I take the wheel, and I am always one step ahead.

<u>Now you're ready to learn to sell.</u>

STAGE #2: YOUR MINDSET

(Understand yourself, to sell to them)

CHAPTER 12

The Key: The space between your ears

> *"Our life is the creation of our mind."*
> *-Buddha*

You must be thinking, *"Cris! Just give me the secrets to manipulate the whole world and sell to 100% of my prospects already!"*

But before beginning to understand how your customers' minds work, you have to learn a little bit more about how your mind works, the mind of a salesman.

How many people have you met that have gotten into sales just to walk out a few months later (with their tails between their legs) saying that *"sales aren't for them?"*

Dozens! If not hundreds! And the truth is that sales are not for everyone, and there is only one reason why you wouldn't like sales: Because you have no idea what you're doing!

By not knowing how to sell, rejection is going to make you its favorite victim.

If even with being rejection's favorite victim you haven't walked out, and you decide to study the psychology of your customers to then be able to sell… You know what's going to push your back up against the wall?

Your own mind!

The salesman's best-kept secret is that every single one of them know their ultimate professional tool is their mind. If somebody messes with your mind, you're done. If somebody occupies space and energy in your head that should be busy with the sale at hand…. You won't make the sale! It's that simple.

Sales is a jealous industry. If you don't have both feet in the game, sales will turn its back on you and send you back to your monotonous office gig.

The best salesmen learn to control and use their minds before trying to control and manipulate (positively) their customers' mind.

You need to know that every inch of your body and your mind will fight exhaustively against you when you try to be successful. Human beings are engineered to seek out comfort, security, and control over everything that surrounds us to minimize risk.

Success requires just the opposite. It requires breaking out of your comfort zone, risking it all, and putting it all on the line. You think that your body will approvingly support you to assume these risks? Of course not!

This is why less than 1% of people you know accomplish true financial abundance.

It's natural to feel frightened, nervous, and to make excuses. Your mind does it automatically for you.

And even if you have crafted a positive relationship with money and you think and speak in terms of abundance, you will continue feeling afraid and terrified of leaving your comfort zone and reaching for the credit card.

And that's why I leave you with the world's greatest lesson:

You are not your thoughts.

Your thoughts can be a thousand things, but they aren't you. You are an upstanding human being, regardless of any opinion or belief. The thoughts going on in your head are information that you have gathered from the outside world. Your brain has processed them through ten thousand filters that you have put up since your childhood.

What is true for you could be a lie to the rest of the world.

Making a million dollars could sound difficult to you, but for thousands of people it's as easy as a snap of the fingers.

Your mind will work against you!

It will tell you to give up, that it's not worth it, that you're too old, that you should rest instead, that you're too tired, that the economy won't let you do it, that it's not your fault, that god has better plans, that right now isn't the best time, that you have a different mission, that you didn't always want it… Your mind will take care of formulating every possible excuse inside you to convince you not to risk it!

An outstanding salesman acknowledges this truth and consciously decides to ignore it and keep pursuing that yes.

Every day, 24/7, 365 days a year.

Even against his own mind.

RECAP:

- You are not your thoughts.

- You're only going to hate selling if you don't know how to do it.

- You are engineered by nature to be comfortable, not to have financial abundance and to realize your maximum potential as a person.

ACTION:

- Identify and throw out your favorite excuses.

In the next list, write down the 10 most common excuses that you've used to avoid doing anything in life.

Examples: It's too late, I don't have the time, I'm tired, now isn't the best time, I'm not ready, what will they say, etc.

MY FAVORITE FALSE EXCUSES:

_____
_____
_____
_____
_____
_____
_____
_____
_____
_____
_____
_____
_____
_____
_____
_____

Now, read the list. Ready? ...Now give yourself a slap in the face for having believed all these excuses until now.

There's no excuse that stands in the way of a truly motivated person!

Identify them and realize that there is always time, other strategies and ways to making things happen.

CHAPTER 13

Open Mind, Closed Mouth

> *"Most people do not listen with the intent to understand; they listen with the intent to reply."*
> -Stephen Covey

Just as in personal finance, the key is spending less than you make; in sales, you must speak less than you listen.

Your goal is not to hypnotize your customer with your voice. Your goal is for them to sell to themselves. Your goal is tempting them to arrive at the conclusion that your product is the right solution to their problem.

You're not able to spoon-feed the right solution to an informed customer, but you are able to tempt them and show them the way so that they convince themselves.

What happens when a salesman doesn't stop talking and the customer never says a word?

The salesman doesn't know where they stand. They don't know if they have a sale or not.

In sales and in life, he who is quiet and listens learns more than he who falls in love with the sound of his own voice.

Don't make the same mistake as the Hawaiian Shirts and listen, listen, listen.

RECAP:

- Listen more, speak much less.

ACTION:

- Make use of open-ended questions.

An open-ended questions' structure encourages your customers to open up to you and speak more. They're questions that are never answered with just a "Yes," "No," or "sometimes" (those are closed-ended questions).

Elaborate several that go ad hoc with your presentation and make use of them today.

Check out the results they give you and how effective they are to making people open up to you.

Examples:

"Mr. Johnson, what are you looking to achieve with this investment?"
"Mrs. Johnson, what do you like the most about family vacations?"
"Mr. Smith, how do you spend your time at home?
"Mrs. Smith, what is the most important thing for you in this purchase?"

- Use the Porcupine Question Technique.

If your customer asks you something related to your product, answer with a question and make them sell themselves the answer.

Example:

Customer: *"Hey Cris, can I bring my 2 cousins to the hotel with this timeshare?"*

You: *"Sir, let me ask you, how important is it for you to travel with more people?"*

Customer: *"Very important! We take my cousins on vacation at least once a year and I'd like to bring my mother-in-law, too."*

You: *"That's great you mention it, Mr. Johnson. I'll show you right away how our membership can work for you and your family."*

So, what did we just witness?

By using these techniques you achieve:

1) Compelling your customer to revisit his priorities relating to your product.

2) Making your customer say aloud that something related to your product is important to him.

3) And most importantly, he starts selling to his wife (if she's sitting next to him).

Mrs. Johnson, sitting at her husband's side, just heard her husband take the initiative regarding your product, ask questions, and give relevance to what you're saying. This will encourage her to ask, too!

Much better results than just answering with "Yes," am I right?

Use this technique this week and notice the results!
AH! I almost forgot… It's called the porcupine technique because, what would be the first thing you do if somebody were to throw a porcupine at you? You'd throw it back! And this is exactly what you do with your customer's question!

CHAPTER 14

Selective Deafness

> *"Humanity's great myth is that a complaint fixes things. Taking action fixes things. One cannot complain and then lay down to sleep."*
> *- Unknown*

The best salespeople are deaf.

Because they DON'T listen to their coworkers' negativity, because they DON'T listen to the fake *"I'm not going to buy anything from you"* that every prospect initially shows as resistance, because they DON'T listen to the excuses that their own minds put forth along the way, and because they don't listen to the 9 NO's they had to filter out to get to one YES.

Remember the wonderful American saying:

"Misery loves company"

Miserable and negative people love to bring you down to their level and justify their mediocrity with your ears. Run away from them!

A great salesman's attitude and emotions are 100% autonomous from the webs of words that pollute the air and their mind.

Learn to make use of selective deafness and defend your production from all the trash floating about in the air... And in the space between your ears.

RECAP:

- Your ability to sell is not dependent upon external factors nor on the obstacles that your mind tosses your way.

- Run away from miserable salespeople; they love to bring you down to their level.

ACTION:

- Identify the "Pity Parties" of your life and run from them.

A "Pity Party" is the worst disease for a salesforce (and for life in general) and unfortunately, they always exist. Identify people who always complain and criticize, who are always sarcastic and say negative things. It doesn't matter if they're friends, family, or even your significant other. It's essential that you take immediate action to make a change in the relationship or to purge them from your life.

Who are they? Write it down below!

Remember that this book is your and your eyes alone. There's no harm done here and anything goes.

MY LIFE'S PITY PARTY IS:

1) _____

2) _____

3) _____

4) _____

5) _____

If you decide to purge people from your life, just do it. You've got nothing to lose and you'll often see your life and your sales much happier and effective without them. This isn't cold or cruel; it's necessary for your success and survival.

If you decide to work on improving the relationship, then clear the air, determine the problem, and lay down expectations which you both can work towards. It'll be difficult, and you have a sea of recently found emotions that's been predicted ahead, but it'll be worth it.

Remember that change is hard at the beginning, messy in the middle, and incredible at the end.

CHAPTER 15

Justification: Human Nature (No to conformity)

"In the republic of mediocrity, genius is dangerous."
-Robert Green Ingersoll

At what point did someone decide that being the best was bad? When did we start seeing people that do anything to reach their goals as people who are ambitious and unbalanced?

We started to when it intimidated us. When the alpha salesman walks in the room, everybody else acknowledges it and the weak step back and justify. This defense mechanism is part of human nature.

You couldn't be number 1? That doesn't give you a reason to justify yourself and discredit the person that did it! When your ego's been hurt is when you truly see how good of a salesman you are. How you handle all the negative feelings that surface makes a world of difference between a good salesman and a bad salesman.

You get resentful, justify the loss, and settle?

Doing this will make you nothing less than a conformist.

Do you positively use that anger to analyze your mistakes, to acknowledge your competition's strengths, and to make sure that you never lose again?

THAT'S THE SPIRIT! That attitude is what'll make you get ahead and keep selling.

And remember that what John says about Peter, speaks more about John than it does about Peter.

Speaking badly about someone just makes you look bad.

And if you do, get the *Hawaiian Shirt* out while you're at it.

RECAP:

- Don't justify your failures, you NEVER lose if you NEVER give up.

- Any criticism you dish out speaks more about you as a person than the object you are criticizing – Be careful! Learn to listen to your subconscious!

ACTION:

* #ZERONEGATIVITY CHALLENGE

The action that you'll be taking today is designed to convey the fact that you win nothing by being negative.

Your challenge will be as follows:

For the next 24 hours you are strictly forbidden to criticize, make fun of, be sarcastic, or speak negatively of any other thing, person, or object.

I encourage you to try this challenge out and I recommend tying a string on your finger to keep it in mind every second of the day.

At the end of the day, write down challenge's results on a sheet of paper, your blog, or Facebook, and share them with us using the hashtag #EverybodySells.

CHAPTER 16

The Biggest Mistake: Underestimation

"If the plan doesn't work, change the plan, but never the goal."

-Unknown

On the pursuit of success, there is only one mistake for why 90% of people fail. That mistake is <u>underestimating.</u>

You have to avoid at all cost having these two problems of underestimation, because if you have them, failure is practically guaranteed.

1) **Underestimating the amount of work necessary to reach your goals and…**

2) **Underestimating the amount of motivation you'll need to extract from your life vision to achieve your goals.**

Work and motivation, effort and energy; it's just that easy.

What happens if you don't calculate exactly how much work it will cost you to achieve your goals? You'll have worked 8 hours per day, 5 days a week for 50 years to end up very far from your original vision.

And what happens if your life vision doesn't motivate you, doesn't excite you, doesn't make you feel passionate? You're going to throw in the towel in after 100 yards… and this is a race of endurance!

That's why you have to devise a life vision that makes you feel passionate and that keeps you awake at night. Then, you have to calculate exactly how much work it will cost you to obtain that life vision and the sacrifices you're willing to make to get it.

Remember that making calculations about the future is one thing alone:

<u>Guessing.</u>

It doesn't matter how much you support your guesses with data. It doesn't make them anything more than a prediction that could be inaccurate.

And the best recommendation you can follow when *guessing* is overestimating. If your goal is $100,000 dollars, focus on producing $300,000, so that if you don't reach the goal, I assure you, you'll be over what you needed.

The only way to not make mistakes in sales and on the path to success is giving 10 times the effort that the average person normally gives.

One of my biggest mentors, *Grant Cardone*, an American real estate millionaire, gets all the credit for teaching me the effectiveness of that saying.

As for estimating the amount of motivation that you'll need to extract from your life vision, we'll address that in chapter 21 (Life Vision and Goals).

RECAP:

- Don't underestimate the amount of work you'll need to reach your goals and life vision. Overestimate! If you want a THOUSAND, go after a MILLION!

- Devise a life vision that makes you feel passionate.

ACTION:

- Reflect.

Take 10 minutes of your day and reflect on how many of your rejections from customers have been due to the lack of effort on your part.

Identify at least 3 instances, and reflect on what you could have done differently.

REFLECT:

Customer #1 that said NO:

_____.

What could I have done differently?

_____
_____
_____
_____

Customer #2 that said NO:

_____.

What could I have done differently?

_____
_____
_____
_____

Customer #3 that said NO:

_____.

What could I have done differently?

_____
_____
_____
_____

CHAPTER 17

Ethics of a Salesman

"Telling the truth and making someone cry is better than telling a lie and making someone smile"

-Paulo Coelho

We've already discussed the mistakes of mediocre salesmen, or *Hawaiian Shirts*, and we mentioned that they tend to see truth as an obstacle. However, this is such an important point in the psychology and mindset of a salesman, that we have to establish clearer ground rules.

You want to know if you're being ethical?

ACTION:

Answer the following questions:

- Do you think that it is sometimes ok to lie in a sale?

- Do you think that it is sometimes ok to leave information out in a sale?
- If you don't know the answer, do you make it up or accept that you don't know?
- Does your product work like you advertise it to?
- Would you buy the product you're advertising?
- If yes, why haven't you already bought it?

If your answer to the first question (Do you think that it is sometimes ok to lie in a sale?) is anything other than NO, I'm sorry to tell you that you're mistaken.

There is no reason that justifies lying to your customers. It is not only ethically lacking, but also a crime and if one of them is smart enough, they'll catch you and pursue legal action. And they're right to do so.

We won't go into detail regarding the other questions, but they're an excellent way to check a salesman's level of ethics. Use them! <u>And remember, every product has their objections, but outstanding salesmen have no need to lie.</u>

RECAP:

- Whatever you do, don't lie or leave out relevant information to your customer, it will follow you to the end of your days.

CHAPTER 18

Neurosis: Nothing is by chance

"Some people create their own storm and then get upset when it rains."

-Unknown

One of the books that's touched my life the most was "The Road Less Travelled" by the American psychiatrist, Scott Peck.

In the book, Dr. Peck describes two disorders that stem from a feeling of responsibility. Dr. Peck describes neurotics as people who take on too much responsibility over the world and their actions, and describes character disordered people as people who have very little feelings of responsibility over the world and their actions.

I've got to tell you, if you have this book in your hands, if you've read it up until this chapter, if you've bothered to learn who I am and to seek to improve your skills in sales...

You're on the neurotic side.

Welcome!

Don't be afraid! It's not what they make it out to be. 99% of the world's biggest accomplishments have been thanks to people who were labeled as: obsessive, maniacal, crazy, intense, workaholics, neurotic, etc. If you don't believe me, read up on Steve Jobs, Mark Zuckerberg, Napoleon Bonaparte, etc.

Who's attached a stigma to terms like obsession, neurosis, and intensity? People who gave up and justified it! The same people who now want you to be one of them!

Being neurotic entails many benefits as a salesman. We're salespeople and we make things happen. We leave nothing to chance, we take action, we pay attention to detail, and we direct our motivation towards carrying out our goals in a quick and agile manner. We hold high expectations and we like to pursue our goals until the end.

Although like everything in this life, neurosis has its defects.

A neurotic, like myself, can reach a point of saturation, of depression, of having trouble delegating and losing focus and losing sight of the importance of their *"Base Reality."*

In my personal story, the biggest problem I've had with my neurosis has been controlling the extent to which I hold myself to high standards. A few years ago I was going through a really stressful time (REALLY STRESSFUL!) at the brink of throwing in the towel, giving up, and moving back in with my parents.

I had huge expectations about what I wanted to achieve in my romantic life, my professional life, and my education… in everything! I wanted to be the superman of productivity.

Although after hitting rock bottom, and after therapy, acceptance, and lots of self-work, I was able to understand that giving your 110% and accepting that not everything will go your way is key to success.

Taking failure personally and getting frustrated isn't good for anything when it's a fundamental part of the game.

There'd be no flavor to sweet without sour.

However, as salespeople, we have to know that no one will do the dirty work for us. We have to embrace (and control) this neurosis in such a way that it pressures us to drive out the best in ourselves.

It's a fine line, but it's fundamental. Because, sorry to burst your bubble, nobody wants to see you triumph more than you! *(and your parents... sometimes!)*. Nothing in this life is free, you have to add value to receive value. You have to practice giving, giving, and giving in order to receive something in exchange.

You have to know that you are the only person that can get things done, and when your success has finally got some momentum, you'll be able to hire more people that you'll sell your life vision to and who will help you build up your dreams.

But, especially at the beginning, if you expect somebody to help you in exchange for nothing …

<u>You'll be waiting for a long time.</u>

RECAP:

- Embrace your neurosis, the greatest salespeople do.

- There's a fine but necessary line between demanding enough from yourself and demanding too much to be successful. Everything's at stake.

ACTION:

- Identify the benefits of your neurosis.

Write below the 5 best and worst things that happen to you when trying to have control, be responsible, obsessive, and neurotic with your profession as a salesman:

5 POSITIVE THINGS ABOUT MY NEUROSIS

_____
_____
_____
_____

5 NEGATIVE THINGS ABOUT MY NEUROSIS

_____
_____
_____
_____

Analyze the pros and cons and work out strategies to minimize the negative side of your neurosis.

CHAPTER 19

Dress for Success: How you look is how you're treated

"If you look good, you feel good, and if you feel good, you do good."

- George St. Pierre

Let's be realistic. We live in a superficial world.

Brand name clothing, cars, trips, resorts, chefs, watches.... It all goes beyond functionality and we pay ridiculously high prices for exclusivity, vanity, and glamour (That's what salespeople like us take care of!).

You don't spend $7,000 dollars on a watch to tell what time it is. You spend $7,000 dollars on a watch so people see you wearing it. We like pretty things, we like things that are similar to us, and this applies as much to watches as it does to people.

Our superficiality even spreads to the people we hang out with and the people we do business with. How we look is how we're treated.

How you physically look tends to be a determining factor for opening doors or getting those first opportunities (in business and in love).

You don't necessarily have to be more beautiful than Emma Watson or more of a ladies' man than Adam Levine, but you do have to invest in how you look so they treat you, well, how you look!

It would seem to simply be common sense... but there are hundreds of people that apparently are aware of, yet decide to ignore, the importance of looking good! And, of course... Common sense is the least common of our senses.

Depending on what you sell and who you sell to, the way you dress will vary. However, always wear clothes that fit you well.

Other than that, here's a few basic, fool-proof rules:

Rule #1 for Personal Appearance:

- *Dress according to the industry, the people, and the occasion.*

You don't know what the dress code is? Find out! Ask around and do research. Always wear clothes you feel comfortable with, but make sure that they're clothes that match the situation. Don't wear a suit that shouts "SALESMAN!" for a more laid-back social gathering. Don't show up with wrinkled or stained clothes or with your shirt untucked. Common sense guys! There's nothing worse than showing up to a social function with start-uppers from California in a Gucci suit, or showing up in a short skirt when meeting with posh old ladies.

Rule #2 for Personal Appearance:

- *Take a personal hygiene kit with you.*

Even worse than showing up badly dressed is showing up badly groomed. Which is exactly why I recommend taking a small kit for personal hygiene with you. Toothbrush, toothpaste, toothpicks, gum, gel, cologne or perfume, and deodorant at the very least. There's nothing that kills a sale faster than a salesman with bad breath. I get sick just thinking about it.

Rule #3 for Personal Appearance:

- *Invest in your appearance.*

It doesn't necessarily have to be expensive clothing, but keep in mind that clothes have a life span, and your dress shirt from your high school graduation, even if it still fits, has already worn out. Go shopping every once in a while.

Rule #4 for Personal Appearance:

- *Don't let your look speak louder than you.*

Unless you sell tattoos, tickets to punk rock concerts, or rock band merchandise – Keep your look conservative. Just as I wouldn't hand over my money to a *Hawaiian Shirt*, I wouldn't hand it over to someone sporting a Mohawk and three nose rings.

Taking care of your personal appearance isn't just a show of respect for your customer. It's also a show of respect for yourself. How do you expect somebody to invest money into someone who doesn't even invest a few bucks into dressing well during office hours?

As the American saying goes…

Dress for Success!

RECAP:

- Your personal appearance and hygiene are fundamental to opening up business opportunities.

- You are the most valuable thing you have! Invest in your appearance!

- If you want to improve how you feel on the inside, improve how you look on the outside.

ACTION:

- Go shopping and buy yourself something tasteful and nice in your customers' eyes.

Yep, that simple. *You loved that action, didn't you?*

CHAPTER 20

Your body language

"Body language is a very powerful tool. We had body language before we had speech!"

- Deborah Bull

<u>93% of communication is non-verbal.</u>

WOW! So words are only 7% of what I convey to my customer?

Right! According to Dr. Albert Merhbian, author of the book "Silent Messages," only 7% of communication are words you say. Your voice tone and other auditory features are 38% of communication, and 55% comes from non-verbal factors (gestures, posture, facial expressions, etc.).

That's why I think it would be worth dedicating some time to studying what a salesman must avoid in terms of body language during a sales pitch or a business meeting.

Touching your face – Other than being considered as an attack on good customs and etiquette, touching your face (any part) inspires distrust among your customers.

Shoulders unaligned with your customer's – The less aligned and farther your shoulders are from your customer's, the more you project a low level of interest in them. The same thing happens with how your feet are angled in comparison to the other person when speaking with someone who's standing.

Scratching your head – You didn't watch cartoons when you were little? Scratching your head is a clear signal that you are seriously unsure about what you are saying. Scratching the back of your head, in particular, indicates insecurity.

Crossing arms over chest – Red flag on all levels. Your customer could think a number of things from A to Z: that you're being defensive, that you're hiding something, that you're in a bad mood, that you don't like them, etc., etc.

Not respecting your customer's personal space – Your personal space starts after shaking someone's hand. I recommend a distance of 4 feet for casual environments, however, I recommend using Edward T. Hall's bubble as a reference on the topic (GOODIES).

Making love to the phone – The ultimate disrespect in this day and age; constantly looking at your cell phone. It projects a lack of attention and disrespect. If you pull your cell phone out during a business meeting or sale, it had better be a real emergency or your spouse telling you you've won the lottery… Because you're not going to make the sale.

Being overly stiff – Looking like a deer in the headlights never helped anybody. Don't freeze up! Your body language ought to be relaxed and subtle. It's better to make a few mistakes than to give the impression of being cold or terrified.

Making eye contact – Eyes are a window to the soul of another. Not making eye contact with your customer projects insecurity and distrust. Your eye contact should be warm and friendly, not tense, inflexible, or outright sinister like a cartoon. Relax.

Your facial expression – It ought to be natural. Anything that you want to emphasize with an expression of the face must be authentic. The most common mistakes are fake smiles and frowning.

ACTION:

To "Audit" how you manage your body language, my best recommendation is to record yourself giving a presentation.

Get your phone's camera and record yourself from head to toe reading an ad pamphlet as if you were trying to make a sale. Afterwards, check the video with another person, friend, or family member. Between the two of you analyze your body language: how you were standing, what you were doing with your hands, whether you were rocking back and forth, where you were looking, what facial expressions you had, how your tone was, etc. Check every point that we just covered in this chapter.

This exercise will give you a really good idea of the things you need to change. You'll realize that they are generally very obvious, and after noticing them once and acknowledging them, you'll easily be able to change them.

I strongly recommend checking not only your body language, but also your intonation, how fast you speak, filler words you may be using, and how clear your voice is. All of these points are important when communicating to your customers.

And bear in mind that if you want to understand your customer better, you have to…

<u>Listen to what they aren't saying.</u>

RECAP:

- Words are only 7% of what you say, the rest is your body language and the tone you use.

- Audit your body language.

GOODIES:

- Check out Edward T. Hall's personal space bubble here: http://www.workingwithcris.com/personalspaceandproxemics/

CHAPTER 21

Motivation

"To be a champ you have to believe in yourself when no one else will."

- Sugar Ray Robinson

If we had to nominate an MVP of every part that makes up the mind of a salesman, without a doubt, we would have to nominate *motivation.*

Do you remember that friend from grade school that had it all to be successful, but just plays Xbox in his parents' basement?

He lacks motivation.

How about that super smart student that never studies for exams?

He lacks motivation, too.

Being motivated is a factor that if lacking, it makes every other quality useless when you want to put them into action.

But what exactly is motivation?

Motivation is a group of internal and external factors that stimulate an individual's desire to be continually interested in a job, object, or situation.

Motivation is built upon the mix of hundreds of factors in your mind. Internal stimuli such as values, priorities, and tastes; and external stimuli such as rewards, social expectations, and conditioning.

Motivation's got an algorithm that's harder to crack than Google's!

And there are dozens of different theories explaining where motivation comes from, and how one can produce it or obtain it. If you want to research in more detail, I recommend reading more about: instinct theory, psychoanalytic theory, and humanist theory. We won't go into it now, because you'd fall asleep immediately.

But what you really have to know as a salesman is that motivation is a different concept for every human being.

Some salespeople are motivated by money, some people by being #1, some people by public recognition, and some people by the look on their children's faces in the morning.

Whatever the factor may be that grants you your motivation, you've got to know that the true salesman doesn't rely upon external stimuli (competition, spiffs, contests, incentives, etc.) in order to sell. They are, of course, an excellent extra push, but a good salesperson doesn't rely on them to be #1.

Of course external competition motivates! But it motivates temporarily. Internal competition is a fire that burns forever!

Tell me who you compete with, and I'll tell you who you are.

That's why outstanding salesmen have the strong tendency to compete more against their own expectations than against their peers. Don't rely on having motivated peers to give the best of you.

Motivation also goes closely hand in hand with general wellbeing that you have as a person. Don't expect to feel 110% if you work all day and never exercise. Don't expect your work to flow easily if you have neglected your family and your significant other.

Motivation, just like success, is holistic and flows better when you've balanced the different areas of your life.

RECAP:

- Motivation is a group of internal and external factors that stimulate an individual's desire to be continually interested in a job, object, or situation.
- Internal competition is a fire that burns forever!
- Motivation flows when one has a general wellbeing or a pressing need.

ACTION:

- Answer and reflect.

What are the things that motivate me to give 110% of myself every morning?

_____
_____
_____
_____

_____

_____

Now, write three success mantras to remind yourself why you do what you do every day. These mantras have to mention some of your motivation sources that you wrote above. You should use them and replay them in your mind every time you need to channel that motivation.

Example.

"<u>Recognition</u> motivates me to be #1."
"My <u>daughter's</u> eyes remind me of the reason I sell."
"I'm a man/woman who improves on a day to day basis!"

My Mantras for Success:

_____
_____
_____
_____
_____
_____

CHAPTER 22

Life Vision and Goals

"Anyone whose goal is 'something higher' must expect someday to suffer vertigo. What is vertigo? Fear of falling? No, Vertigo is something other than fear of falling. It is the voice of the emptiness below us which tempts and lures us, it is the desire to fall, against which, terrified, we defend ourselves"
- Milan Kundera

For years I was in charge of recruitment in the sales area for one of the biggest hospitality companies in the world, and it was an impressive life lesson:

<u>Human resources aren't easy... and less so with salesmen.</u>

Why? Because an interview is nothing more than a sales presentation of yourself! And when you interview salespeople, they try (sometimes terribly) to spoon-feed you what they think you want to hear.

But there's one question that takes down even the best salesman's bluff:

Where do you see yourself personally and professionally in the next 5 to 10 years?

It's a basic question! I know! But 99% of the answers I've gotten are:

"Working in your company!"

"In your position!"

"Being successful in the position I'm applying for!"

Why do I say that this shoots down the candidate's bluff?

Because everybody forgot to mention where they saw themselves personally!

Even when I dug deeper and asked the question directly, very few candidates could determine where they wanted to be personally in 5 or 10 years' time. Not even vague answers!

And if you can't answer that question… Who can?

Having a clear life vision is a key element to staying self-motivated, full of energy, and running in the right direction. Without a life vision, where are you going to go?

As you've already created your own definition for success in chapter 5, you already have an exact idea of what success is for you and you know where priorities in life lie. This was the first step to now create an incredible life vision.

Remember that your definition of success is one thing, and your life vision is something totally different. Your definition of success will clear your mind so you're able to determine what you want in life. Alternatively, your life vision will help lead the way to getting the success you've already defined. They are complementary and sequential, but not the same thing.

To start creating your life vision, I recommend following the same procedure that I apply and use every day. It's important to know if you run to the internet and search this topic, every person, "guru," or individual will have a different technique. Some of them can be very far-fetched in my opinion; which is exactly why my method is very simple.

ACTION:

Note: You're going to need a pen and paper! Or even better, download the Excel spreadsheet (check out the GOODIES).

1) <u>Determine what you want to achieve in 5, 10, and 20 years professionally, emotionally, spiritually, physically, and financially.</u>

   Now is the time to be specific. Have your definition of success at your side and use it as reference for every word you write, to make sure that what you want to achieve in life is congruent with what you deem successful.

   Feel free to add any other area that's very important to you. Generally speaking, professional, emotional, spiritual, physical, and financial factors tend to cover everything; but for example, if a life goal for you is to be the best amateur cook in your city, you could add it.

   It's your life! You decide.

To make this even easier to understand, below I have attached an example:

	What can I do TODAY?	**5 years**	**10 years**	**20 years**
Professional	Call 50 prospects. Review my commercial strategy.	That my company surpasses 100,000 satisfied customers	That my company is listed in the New York stock market.	Have sold my company and started a new venture.
Emotional	Make dinner for my significant other, enjoy, and show them how much they matter to me.	Get married to the woman of my dreams, working towards creating a realationship based on love and support every day. Doing so by knowing well who it is I am	Have children with the woman of my dreams and raise a family. While looking out for my emotional wellbeing in order to support them.	Have responsible, happy children who are true to themselves. Have a life partner who I can serve and support on a daily basis and a relationship where love and support are priority.
Spiritual	Meditate 20 minutes. Book a spiritual retreat for this year	Having constantly meditated (at least half the year) for a given period of time. Having attended 3 spiritual retreats.	Meditate daily and pass this tool on to my children and family.	Manage to help the world through my spiritual experience and guidance.
Physical	Run 10 kilometers and create a healthy meal plan for the week.	Run a marathon and do exercise 5 times a week. Watch my diet every day.	Do an Ironman triathlon. Do exercise 5 times a week. Watch my diet every day.	Break a sport's world record. Do exercise 5 days a week. Watch my diet every day.

Financial	Call 50 prospects for my company today. Review my business's scalability.	Have $1,000,000 in cash.	Have $10,000,000 in cash.	Have $100,000,000 in cash.

This table will be your key tool to prove that you are on a good path in life, on a daily basis. You have to check this table and update your "What can I do today" column! Every day!

Doing so will allow you to clarify your priorities of today and never to lose focus of where you wish to be. Remember that each of your goals, whatever the deadline, have to be strongly emotionally charged. They have to be goals that excite you. Dare to dream and ignore the excuses that your mind throws in your way!

And as always, remember that success changes, and that if someday you find yourself needing to change a goal, first ask yourself:

Why do I want to change this goal? Do I truly want to change it? Do I no longer want the benefits that come with? Or did I just lose motivation? What made me lose my motivation? Can I recover it?

If every one of these questions confirm that this goal is no longer priority, get rid of it, toss it out, and create a new vision.

Now you have a life vision!

You already know why you are selling, and your motivation will be dependent upon no one other than you!

Congratulations!

RECAP:

- If you don't know the reason you sell for, then who does?
- Personal definition of Success + Life vision = the right path to build on, sell on, and to reach all of your goals on.
- Creating your life vision is easy and simple!

GOODIES:

*Get your Life Vision Organizer here:

http://www.workingwithcris.com/lifevisionorganizer3

STAGE #3: YOUR CUSTOMER'S MINDSET

(Understanding their mind and closing the sale)

CHAPTER 23

80% human, 20% product

"The great gift of human beings is that we have the power of empathy."
- Meryl Streep

If we had to take a salesman's brain and divvy up exactly what percentage should work to store knowledge, we'd have to leave 80% of space to store knowledge about human beings and 20% for knowledge about the product.

It doesn't matter if you sell cheese, insurance, homes, timeshares, cars, planes, or tours; you're not in that industry. You're in the human being industry, and to be able to sell in that industry you have to focus on them. You have to take care of them and want what's best for them.

For that reason, all of stage 3 of this book is devised for you to learn and get to know which behavioral patterns make the human being playing the role of "customer" so irrational, emotional, and wonderful. At the same time, you'll learn to use these patterns to sell to them as well as improving the size of your customer base. Take note and apply everything!

Remember that you can know your product 100% and know its every detail, but if you don't know how a human being's mind works, you won't be able to make the sale!

RECAP:

- You're in the human being industry, not in your product's.

ACTION:

- You're still applying every single one of this book's actions, right?

You're growth is only dependent on this! Apply and practice!

CHAPTER 24

Communicating with Your Customer (Filters)

"Lose your ego and find yourself."
- Debra Roberts

Communication is not easy.

It's the main reason for problems, including divorce, war, and fights to the death among drunks in a bar. Most humans don't know how to express what we want or feel and we don't know how to listen to others and understand their point of view either.

And all of this is due to our old friend, the EGO.

The most important thing for a human being is themself. Not you, not your plans, your conversations or ideas on the world. It's them, their dreams and their initiatives.

And your ability to sell relies on your ability to understand them.

A very important point to starting to be empathetic with your customers and truly putting yourself in their shoes is that you understand what communication filters are.

I'll use a clear example of my years in timeshares to show this to you.

A salesman goes walking around a hotel with a guest during his sales pitch.

"When you travel, Mr. Johnson, how many days do you usually travel for?" the salesman asked.

"Well, I always travel for short periods of times, 2 or 3 nights at the most," Mr. Johnson replied.

Here the average salesman, would immediately assume that since their timeshare program only allows reservations for full vacations, the customer will have that objection. He makes this assumption because it has happened to him repeatedly, because his experience says so.

On the other hand, an outstanding salesman would assume nothing, wouldn't filter out information through his experience, and would keep asking:

"How come Mr. Johnson? Why such short trips?"

"Ugh, for work more than anything, but I'll retire soon and it will be time for a bit more rest."

Cha-ching! Cha-ching!

The smell of money is in the air and everything's just peachy, because you just skipped an huge objection that would have required energy and time, with just asking a bit more.

So remember that, in every process of communication, you're filtering out what the other person says through your personal experience and sales experience. You can't allow the filters to send you in the wrong direction.

Never assume, always ask.

RECAP:

- Every human being filters out communication according to their life experiences.

- Never assume, always ask.

ACTION:

- Identify 3 instances when assumptions have cost you a sale. Afterwards, identify what information you needed to have and what question would have given it to you.

Instance #1:
_____
_____

What question would have helped me to save the sale?
_____
_____

Instance #2:
_____
_____

What question would have helped me to save the sale?
_____
_____

Instance #3:
_____
_____

What questions would have helped me to save the sale?
_____
_____

Make use of these cases to identify your recurring mistakes and from now on always ask!

CHAPTER 25

Emotional purchases, logical justifications

"We can be masters of our thoughts but we will always be slaves to our emotions."
- Unknown

You probably still remember when your grade school teacher told you that the difference between humans and animals is our highly developed ability to reason.

This famous ability to reason is what makes us analyze what actions are good or bad, classify them, and therefore defend ourselves. It's the same ability that makes us want to improve upon our reality, and make shortcuts to live in a more protected and comfortable fashion.

But if we had to define human beings into just one word, I would in no way use "rational."

Because even if we are a bit more advanced than other types of animals,

We remain a highly illogical and irrational species!

And we're irrational thanks to the factor that truly characterizes us:

That we are emotional beings.

Emotions override logic. When emotions enter the equation, logic tends to fade to the background. That's exactly why you had a long distance relationship at 16. It's exactly why Mr. Smith gambled his house in the casino. And it's exactly why Kim Kardashian got butt implants.

We act illogically based on how we feel, on how things make us feel, or on how we think they will make us feel.

And what is a sale if not an exchange of emotions? An exchange of energy from one person to the other?

When you learn to convey emotion to others is when you learn to sell.

And that brings us to this chapter's lesson:

People make emotional purchases, and logical justifications.

People always buy out of emotion.

People buy for: how the salesman made me feel, how I'll feel when my neighbors see me in this car or these clothes or this watch, and how creativity will flow through my fingertips when I get that new Macbook... Feelings are everything!

There will be times where you have an extremely logical customer who will want everything to make mathematical sense in order to make a purchase. In these cases, work with them, show them the numbers, but never forget that the drop that will make the credit card glass overflow is emotion.

We all want to feel good. We all want to be better and for people to acknowledge it.

And if your product gives me that, I'm going to buy it right now.

How do you make sure to convey emotion to your customers?

Through pictures, stories, voice tone, details, descriptions, examples, visuals, videos, etc.

Everything that can be digested through your eyes and ears can cause excitement!

It's your job to make these emotions positive and for them to encourage the purchase.

Once you've understood this, it's time to move on to the other side: Days after your customer already bought from you.

Your customer bought from you in a rush of adrenaline, emotion, happiness, and excitement.

Days after this rush, this dose of feel-good, it will pass. Suddenly the "new" is "old" and my beloved salesman isn't here to make me feel the reasons of why I bought this product.

What happens then?

Your customer will try to justify their purchase with logic, with data, and information.

Nobody wants to look like a fool when making a purchase decision. Nobody wants to regret a financial decision, and it's your job to give your customer enough printed, audio, video, or whatever-type of information, so that days later, they themselves justify their purchase.

This feeling of regret after making a purchase is called *"Buyer's remorse."*

And how do I avoid buyer's remorse and that my customer doesn't want to cancel on me?

I follow up and give enough information to justify their decision along with the price paid.

And even more importantly: I sell them a product that actually is useful.

At this stage, your product's reputation is very important because nothing sends a sale up in smoke faster than a bad online reputation.

Nothing scares a customer more than seeing their treasured purchase ripped apart in a thousand pieces on the internet with horror stories.

<u>Take care of your reputation, follow-up, and provide information that justifies the purchase!</u>

RECAP:

- Your customer purchases emotionally and justifies logically.

ACTION:

- Create an anti-cancelation plan.

Create an anti-cancelation plan for your product. The most effective plans always follow a post-purchase touchpoint structure between the seller and customer.

Maybe a simple call for feedback and thanks a few days later, sending a thank you gift for their purchase, installation assistance and first month servicing, weekly reports on results, etc. etc.

Find a way to provide the information that your customer needs, to justify their purchase even when the initial excitement is no longer present.

CHAPTER 26

VISUALS: Don't tell them, show them

"Credibility is a basic survival tool."
- Rebecca Solnit

Accept it. Your customer doesn't trust you.

They have no reason to. You're a salesman and the only thing you want is their money, right? You're after them and you'll do anything to get into their wallet and take everything, down to the last cent! You're evil and overbearing!

Right?

Probably not (And if so, please go back and read chapter 7). But this is what your customer thinks of you before getting to know you.

By nature, your customer will get defensive and won't trust you and your words.

But you know what your customer does place their trust in?

Everything you have in writing.

By having something in writing about a company or person, they can be held responsible for the product it advertises and sells. It's a big liability as a salesman. However, it's the least you can do to take care of your customer and make them feel confident about what they're doing.

People are very visual and attribute much value to what's in writing. That's precisely why you have to have absolutely everything you promise in writing.

And not with pen or pencil! Printed on good quality letterhead paper with your logo, name, and everything you can do to show more formality.

Don't miss out on a sale for not having things in writing.

RECAP:

- People place their trust in what you have in writing, not in your words.

ACTION:

- Double check all of your product's stationery.
  Make sure that you have abundant stock and that you are never short.

CHAPTER 27

Your customer's EGO

"Everything needed to get rid of one's ego is awareness"
- Unknown

And we're back to the **ego**.

<u>But what is the ego and why is it so important in sales?</u>

The ego is our self-image, the image we all have of ourselves. It's the image and story that a human being attributes to themselves, to be unique and to justify their self-worth.

The ego, though highly criticized by spiritual gurus, has good and bad sides, like everything in this life. It's up to us to know how to control it and observe it, from a healthy perspective.

Though in sales, your biggest concern is that:

    A) Your customer's ego is praised.
    B) Your ego and that of your customer do not clash.

A very common mistake in sales is assuming an arrogant attitude, due to possessing all this knowledge about manipulating another person. You have to be very careful with this. It's easy to get your head in the clouds when you managed to close a miraculous sale and your wallet gained 30 pounds.

Oftentimes, an arrogant salesman runs into an arrogant customer, rapport never materializes, and the only one who ends up losing is the salesman.

An outstanding salesperson prioritizes their customer's ego and learns to manage their own from a (smarter) point of view with humility and service.

<u>Don't let your ego get in the way. It's just another one of your mind's strategies to make things harder along your path to success… Take care!</u>

RECAP:

- Don't let your ego get in the way.
- Your customer's ego is priority.

ACTION:

- Reflect

Remember the toughest customer that you've spoken to, the customer that you disliked the most and whom you obviously couldn't sell to.

Now ask yourself: Had I managed MY EGO differently, how could I changed things around?

CHAPTER 28

Fear of Losing (Loss Aversion)

"Why is it so hard to detach from things?"
- Unknown

The possibility of losing stirs up almost twice as much emotion as the possibility of winning.

That's why you see people doing so much more to not lose two dollars, than to earn 100. That's exactly why the world spends its days saving pennies instead of focusing on producing more money.

Why? Because producing more involves effort and risk. Saving just involves not losing, not moving, and staying safe. Being stationary is much easier and looks safer. When in reality, staying stationary ensures the devaluation of one's value sooner or later. Moving and taking risks makes us fight to grow in value.

The father of behavioral economics, Daniel Kahneman, has proven this behavior through hundreds of experiments and has bestowed an excellent tool upon salesman to sell and understand human beings a little bit better.

ACTION:

- Apply loss aversion in your sales process.

Examples:

You could start by narrowing it down to limited-time offer: *"Mr. Johnson! This price is only good up until next Friday, <u>after that date you would miss out on the sale and the super discount!</u>"*

Or you could apply this knowledge in your general communication (written or verbal): *"Mr. Smith, you can't miss out on this opportunity"* instead of *"Mr. Smith, you would gain so much with this opportunity."*

<u>Don't miss out on loss aversion to sell more! Do you know how much money you're leaving on the table? All the commissions you're losing?</u>

(Hint hint, see what I did there?)

RECAP:

- Your customer will do more to not lose than to win.

CHAPTER 29

Need for Closu-

"Curiosity is not a sin. But we should exercise caution with our curiosity."
- Albus Dumbledore

Your mind read "Closure" in the title, am I right?

As human beings we tend to classify everything and want to control everything that surrounds us.

What happens when something is inconclusive? When we missed out on the end of a story? On seeing the last half of the movie? Or on the joke's punchline?

Curiosity kills us! And emotion then kicks into gear.

Keep this in mind when you're negotiating with your customer. Your goal during your sales pitch is to keep your customer intrigued and interested in what you have to say. Therefore, structure your words, your stories, and the information that you give, gradually accumulating. Build up tension to arrive at a grand resolution.

Leave the best for last, build up (positive) tension, and always tempt your customers.

Tempt them to inquire, to get to know more, to find out the reasons and the details. Don't hand over all the information at once, try to get them to be the ones asking.

This factor also applies to printed communication (copywriting), craft your wording in a way that tempts people and encourages them to act.

And most importantly on this matter:

The factor that all salesmen have to know to close 100% of their people is th-

RECAP:

- Your customer needs closure.

- Tempt them to inquire.

- Create your sales pitch in a way that gradually builds up.

ACTION:

- Structure your pitch in in a way that gradually builds up.

Temptingly encourage your customers to inquire and to know more. Tell stories, and do it starting today.

CHAPTER 30

Your customer wants what they don't have and what they admire

"It is in the character of few to honor, without envy, a friend who has prospered."
- Aeschylus

The Rolling Stones said it the best:

"You can't always get what you want
but if you try sometimes,
well you might find,
you get what you need"

We all want what we don't have!

It's a basic law in life. But why is the grass always greener on the other side?

There are three behaviors of your customer's mind that explain why they want what they can't have:

1) **Heightened Attention:** When someone "can't" have something, their brain immediately starts paying more attention to this forbidden object. This is due to our ego being hurt since we can't buy or have something for some reason.

2) **Perceived scarcity (or exclusivity):** When someone "can't" have something, their mind associates it to this product's scarcity and that people that have it are special and different. And, obviously, we all want to be special and different.

3) **Psychological Rebellion:** We hate being told what we can and can't do. Human beings are stubborn by nature and this will make you want something even more.

On the other hand, your customer also wants to have what people who they admire have.

That's why celebrity endorsements are so successful.

You want to be like Michael Jordan? Buy a pair of Nike shoes!

You want to be like George Clooney? Drink Nespresso!

You want to be like Jason Statham? Drive an Audi!

We all want to imitate people that we believe reflect our definition for success, or who we see are admired by many and who possess recognition, glamor, and money.

Your customer is no exception!

Show them that people like them are buying your product to elevate their quality of life. Show them testimonials and even introduce them to other satisfied customers.

RECAP:

- Your customer wants what they can't have.
- Your customer wants what people who they admire have.

ACTION:

- Learn to use this technique today.

You could use reverse psychology and tempt your customer into wanting something by thinking that you don't have it available.

Example: *"Mr. Smith, unfortunately the model you want isn't in stock now. However, if I were to make it happen, do we have a deal?"* Just make sure you make your customer commit and that you do indeed have the product (duh!).

A risky technique that requires a careful hand would be to ask your customer how much they plan on spending on the product they're looking for. Once they establish an amount, make sure they see a product that costs more than they were planning on spending.

If they ask, answer tactfully, *"Mr. Smith, you've got good taste! However, this product is over your budget, let me show you an alternative."*

You must be careful with this technique. It tends to be very effective in making your customer spend a bit more. We all want what we don't have and even more so if someone tell us we can't.

CHAPTER 31

The value of a referral

> *"The money's in referrals!"*
> *- An intelligent salesman*

A recommendation is worth its weight in gold.

Why's that? Because it grants instant credibility (depending on who referred you)!

If you just closed a deal with a renowned businessman, his word and influence will be your best friends. Make him commit to referring and recommending you, provided that your service is the best that he has received in his life.

Always have a referral format ready for your customers and use it when your customer is most enamored with you and your product. Use it when they're most excited and would want to recommend you to their friends.

In your customer's mind, this has two purposes: One, being able to show off what he bought to his friends, and that he has money; and two, he will justify his purchase by recommending it to all of his friends.

In your mind, this has one meaning:

You close more than 50%, depending on your product, and much, much more money.

RECAP:

- A recommendation is worth its weight in gold.

- A list of referrals (a plus on the website)

ACTION:

-Make a referral list and start asking for them TODAY!

CHAPTER 32

Faster horses

"If I had asked people what they wanted, they would have said faster horses." – Henry Ford

People don't know what they want until you show them.

Don't assume the customer necessarily knows what they need (Remember? Assume nothing!).

Often, especially when your product is new and innovative, it will be necessary to educate your market.

It's a highly difficult mission. But if accomplished, it has impressive results, since you'll be the only salesman with a unique product that will revolutionize your industry.

What's important here is a humble approach. Nobody wants to do business with a know-it-all who comes in to interrupt what's already set in place, and nor do they want to do business with an entrepreneur who doesn't convey confidence.

Firstly, I recommend communicating appreciation and admiration for your customer's culture and way of doing things. This will lower their defenses, stroke their ego, and will manage to open up doors so that they listen to you. After this, make sure to have all the necessary information developed visually, concretely, and in a way that's easy to digest, to then go over with your customers.

When elaborating your printed material (and also when you're writing up your sales pitch) always tweak your wording by asking the following questions:

What benefit is my customer searching for with my product? Will this sentence emphasize said benefit?

If it doesn't, get rid of it. You don't want whole paragraphs. You want concrete points of easily digested information that grabs your customer's attention and tempts them. Only then will you be able to educate your customer.

Be empathetic with your customer when educating them, and be knowledgeable about your product and industry to make your proposal much more accepted.

Don't be scared to innovate, but don't come off as an overbearing extremist like Che Guevara or as a confused start-upper.

RECAP:

- Customers don't always know what they need.
- Educating your customer is a complicated art.

ACTION:

- Write out your sales pitch.

Write out word for word what you're going to say when you have a customer in front of you. Divide it up into sections and important points that you need to express. Fine-tune it and read it over and over before the meeting.

CHAPTER 33

AGREE: Your customer is always right (even if they aren't)

"There's nothing more important in a sale than agreeing with your customer about everything. Yes, everything.
- Grant Cardone

This is going back a bit to the topic of leaving your ego aside and making your client a priority. Your ego can't get in the way during the sales process.

What happens if you don't agree with somebody?

You create conflict with them.

Yeah, conflict is a strong word, but it doesn't matter how polite you are, how good of a communicator you are. When you minimize somebody's opinion, you enter into conflict, and there isn't a worse emotional state to make a sale in than conflict.

Your customer doesn't want to negotiate with people that contradict them.

Your customer wants to negotiate to people like him or her!

Think about it, who are you best friends in life?

Your best friends in life are people that you agree with in the topics that are most relevant to you!

Topics like relationships, friendship, life, politics, education, family, entertainment, etc. All of these topics are the perfect grounds to work on building up rapport with your customer.

"Cris, but what happens if my customer says something really stupid? Or what if my customer says LOADS of stupid things?"

Great question! Because it will happen. Not all customers are the nicest and smartest people in the world.

When you customer says something that you completely disagree with, you still have to agree. Your verbal, body, and facial expressions can never show rejection. You have to agree with the fact that they have the right to hold that opinion. Not with what they said, but that they have the liberty to express themselves.

It's not the time to show off your ego and to strut it around while educating your customer on their life perspective. It's the time to educate them on your product and sell. That's it, that's your end goal.

Don't let your ego distract you.

RECAP:

- Your customer wants to do business with people that make them feel good.

- Your most important relationships are with people that you agree with the most.

- Never go into conflict, always let them have the last word.

ACTION:

- #IGNOREYOUREGO CHALLENGE

    For one day, ignore the need to correct people or give advice that wasn't asked for in your personal life (not in sales). People often do not appreciate these pieces of advice or your ego's interruptions in correcting them.

Focus on letting people be and not getting involved for 24 hours. Look at it like a 24-hour rest for the little neurotic inside of you, and afterwards, assess your results and share them with me via Facebook or Twitter.

CHAPTER 34

Got haters?

> *"Love your haters. They're your biggest fans."*
> *- Kanye West*

In the process of creating your life vision and finding your definition for success, you're going to encounter a psychological phenomenon of humankind that you will have to know how to overcome.

They're known as *Haters*.

What are they? Haters are people that attack you through jokes, sarcasm, or parody trying to ridicule your efforts to living your life to the fullest or doing things in a certain way. Haters come in all types of packaging and there's no signage that tells you where you'll find them.

Starting today, what do haters mean for you?

Haters are a sign of success. A sign that you're doing something right.

Let's get to understand the term a little better. The existentialist philosopher, Søren Kierkegaard, (who was born more than 100 years ago), excellently explains this Haters phenomenon.

"There is a form of envy of which I frequently have seen examples, in which an individual tries to obtain something by bullying. If, for instance, I enter a place where many are gathered, it often happens that one or another right away takes up arms against me

by beginning to laugh; presumably he feels that he is being a tool of public opinion.

But lo and behold, if I then make a casual remark to him, that same person becomes infinitely pliable and obliging. Essentially it shows that he regards me as something great, maybe even greater than I am: but if he can't be admitted as a participant in my greatness, at least he will laugh at me. But as soon as he becomes a participant, as it were, he brags about my greatness."

A hater is someone who feels intimidated by your way of living or something in particular. You have no reason to feel offended. Your ego is not part of this battle.

Your ego has to see beyond, operate from a perspective 10,000 feet above, where you don't involve yourself in such earthly matters such as hating. Without fail, criticism says more about the critic than the criticized. Each of our critics are reflections of our insecurities, fears, or frustrations.

What do I recommend doing with haters?

Sell to them, of course.

First, treat them with love. Speak with them, take a casual approach (never complaining – this just feeds the hating) and try to make them part of your journey. Try to convert them into a tool for your success. Ask for help with some task or another where you know they are capable. Acknowledge some of their talents, and tell them that you think they could greatly contribute to the project that you're developing.

Find the way to validate them. Give them recognition.... Even if there isn't much to recognize.

Never succumb to provocation. You are 10,000 feet in the air negotiating and selling yourself the life that you deserve. They're stuck on the floor... intimidated.

RECAP:

- Haters are inevitable, they're a sign of success.
- Haters are tools for your growth.
- Work 10,000 feet in the air, not on ground level.

ACTION:

- Earn yourself a hater.

    Identify your most intense hater today, and sell them the idea of being at your side, of being part of your path to success.

CHAPTER 35

"People don't like to be sold, but they love to buy."
- Jeffrey Gitomer

Not a single more powerful sentence exists in your education as a salesman than this one:

Your customer hates to be sold, but loves to buy.

So what do *you* have to do as a salesman?

Turn into a buying assistant!

Stop thinking of your job as manipulating someone until you get them to buy what you decide is best for them. Turn yourself into a trustworthy advisor, into someone who standing in the shoes of your customer in order to truly help them choose the best product to solve their problem and the best product for their wallet.

Why does your customer hate to be sold?

Because when someone "sells you," they make you feel like as if you didn't have an ounce of control. You feel manipulated. Simply, it makes you feel bad!

Analyze your best sales. It's not common for the customer to say "I was sold." Everyone justifies the sale saying "I just bought X" or "I just invested in an X."

Always let your goal be a customer that felt in control of the negotiation. A customer that never saw you acting like a salesman… Even if you had.

RECAP:

- Your customers hate to be sold, but love to buy.
- Make them feel 100% in control.

CHAPTER 36

Weakness to opportunity

> *"Rather than love, than money, than fame, give me truth."*
> *- Henry David Thoreau*

Everything in this life has good and bad sides to it (as we saw in Chapter 8 when talking about the *Hawaiian Shirt* mistakes).

iPhones are terrific tools: user-friendly, have a million apps to do everything, and are beautifully designed.... But the battery life is a nightmare.

A Porsche is a heck of a car: fast, elegant, and sophisticated... but the car's clearance is a nightmare. Going over even the smallest bump is nearly impossible.

The internet has revolutionized the world and the way we communicate and get information... It's incredible! But it also has brought about too much information, too much anonymity, and too much noise.

Everything in life has a positive and negative side. It's yin and yang, the eternal balance of this world.

And just as iPhones, Porsches, and the Internet aren't perfect... You and your product aren't either.

Don't try to sell your customer the "perfect" product. Your customer isn't stupid and knows when things are sounding too good to be true.

Your job as a salesperson is to be aware of your products weaknesses; to know what it can and can't do, and know how to utilize and present this information.

There's no worse mistake than lying about your product's weaknesses. It is simply unacceptable! You have to recognize your product's weaknesses and use them to sell. If your product's qualities are good, sufficiently good, one weakness will not derail a sale. It will actually add credibility to the product.

ACTION:

* Apply this today.

For example:

"Mr. Smith, as I'm sure you have already realized, this property isn't in the best neighborhood in town. It's in a very quiet, middle-class area. However, I think exactly that makes it a great opportunity. At this price, and with this square footage and the apartment's incredible design, it's the best opportunity I've seen in years. Don't you agree?"

Notice how in this case I described the product's weakness (the bad neighborhood) without saying a single negative word. I didn't say "it's in a bad neighborhood," I said "it's not in the best neighborhood" and immediately proceeded to explain why this weakness is actually the biggest opportunity for the customer.

Note how at the end I didn't ask "What do you think?" I asked, "Don't you agree?" This question will force your customer to give a yes or no so we will know exactly where they stand and how important this weakness may be for them. If the no is firm, you'll save yourself the time and look at other properties for him; if a "yes…" is the answer, you might just have a sale.

Here the important thing is that you take control of your product's weaknesses, and that you're the first to mention them. When your customer mentions the weaknesses first, they'll feel as if they owned that criticism and take it much more seriously than if you had mentioned it first.

RECAP:

- Everything in life has a good side and a bad side.
- Use your product's weaknesses to sell more.
- Mention weakness before your customer does.

CHAPTER 37

Best-selling emotions

> *"Emotion is energy in motion."*
> *- Peter McWilliams*

We humans are a mess of emotions. Some more than others of course, but as we've already seen before, being emotional is our core characteristic as a species.

And just so you have an idea of how wide the emotional spectrum is, when speaking with your customer, he or she could be experiencing any of the following emotions: happiness, sadness, courage, jealousy, envy, hate, pain, affection, love, fear, embarrassment, resentment, guilt, rage, amazement, disgust, desire, indifference, boredom, peace, insecurity, serenity, curiosity, passion, braveness, optimism, deception, rebellion, and much more.

The range of emotions that a human can experience is TREMENDOUSLY wide!

But do you know what the magic of all of this is? That, even though you already know it, it's not necessary to learn a great deal about every single emotion that you are capable of as a human being.

There are certain emotions that are more purchase-motivating than others:

Greed: "If I buy now, I'll be rewarded more!"
Fear: "If I don't buy now, I'll be in trouble!"
Altruism: "If I buy now, I'll help others!"

Envy: "If I don't buy now, the competition will beat me!"
Pride: "If I buy now, I'll look smarter and it'll be noticed!"
Shame: "If I don't buy now, they'll think I'm stupid!"

80% of your customers' decisions will be based on these 6 emotions and it's very important to determine which emotion or which combination thereof you'll use with each customer.

How do you determine this?

Getting to know you customer well!

You have to know what your customer's belief system is, what they love, what's important to them, what they relate to, and at the same time, what they hate and what is a low priority for them. Once you get this information from your customer, you have to be very specific to really get the emotions to surface.

If you know that your customer's main competitor is a corporate monster like Microsoft, use that company as reference so that the emotion that you wish to create is more real.

ACTION:

- Apply it TODAY.

Example –

"Mr. Smith, you know Microsoft well. Their resources are virtually limitless and are always growing. However, my product gives you the first play in a new competitive field where Microsoft still is in

diapers. You'll take the first step in this field and be rewarded for it."

Which emotions were put into play there?

Pride: "If I buy now, I'll look smarter and it will be noticed!"
Shame: "If I don't buy now, they'll think I'm stupid!"
Envy: "If I don't buy now, the competition will beat me!"

At the least!

The more emotions that are activated in your pitch, the better your results will be.

RECAP:

- Humans' range of emotion is tremendously wide.

- There are 6 emotions that close 80% of sales.

- Get to know your customer and be specific when selling.

CHAPTER 38

How to Give Advice that Goes Somewhere

> *"Take my advice, I don't actually use it anyway."*
> *- Unknown*

How many times have you given excellent advice just to find out that your customer did just the opposite?

I bet more than once.

But why?! When we met, everything was crystal clear. I told him not to do exactly what he did and he agreed. What went wrong?

It's not your fault, don't worry. It's simply a fact that the percentage of people that follow advice is extremely low. Why is that? Because your ego tells us that we have a better solution, that if we follow our instinct we'll head down the right path (which most of the time is completely false).

To make that not happen again, here's the solution.

People very rarely accept, follow, and execute advice (much less from a salesman), but people will always emulate success stories.

Don't simply give your customer something to read. Tell them a success story that inspires them and that will motivate them to act.

The lesson you want to give your customer can't end up in their mind like, *"My salesman recommended that I do this."* It has to end up in their mind as, *"There's an incredible instance of a person doing exactly this and they got incredible results."*

People follow examples wherever they see positive results and will listen more to stories or testimonials from people that were already in their shoes.

Use this and start giving advice that goes somewhere.

RECAP:

- People don't follow advice, they follow examples and stories.
- Change the way in which you educate your customers.

ACTION:

- Find two success stories related to your product.

Write them down on the next page as if you were conversing with someone. That way you'll have the exact vocabulary at hand to be able to tell your customers about it. Double check which emotions you are trying to activate with each story and clearly develop them.

Success Story #1:

_____
_____
_____
_____
_____
_____
_____
_____
_____
_____
_____

Success Story #2:

_____
_____
_____
_____
_____
_____
_____
_____
_____
_____

Success Story #3:

_____
_____
_____
_____
_____
_____
_____
_____
_____

CHAPTER 39

Objections and How to Shoot Them Down

"If we had to analyze every single one of the universe's objections before trying something, we would never do anything."
- Samuel Johnson

There are two reasons for why sales pay so well:

1) Because we're told NO every day (and this is emotionally taxing) and
2) For the masterful skill of fighting objections.

We will visit the first point (handling rejection) in the next chapter. In this chapter we'll talk about objections.

Here you have the most common reactions from a mediocre salesman (a *Hawaiian Shirt*) when they lose the sale for not knowing how to handle an objection:

1) *"Dang it, I didn't see that objection coming."*
2) *"Again with the same objection!"*
3) *"Really? As if I already didn't already know that objection..."*

You want to avoid number one? Anticipate the objection!
You want to avoid number two? Analyze and practice your objections!
You want to avoid number three? Keep on selling!

Objections are a natural part of a sale. They are a headache for many salespeople and your ability to handle them determines if you show up to work taking public transportation or driving a

Porsche (and if public transportation doesn't motivate you to learn to handle them, nothing will!).

But what exactly is an objection?

Many salesman will tell you that an objection is a customer on the run, that it's a customer playing hard to get and guarding their money. Or that it's a customer who's not really interested.

But the truth is that…

An objection is just a request for more information.

It's not rocket science, and it's really not that complicated.

When a customer raises an objection, they are asking you to give them more information: to add value to your product and for you to validate that they are making a smart decision by investing their money with you.

The most interesting aspect about objections is that it doesn't matter what industry you're in or what product you're selling. They tend to repeat themselves. I bet that you've heard these objections even if you sell chocolate or private jets:

1) It's too expensive.
2) I need to think about it.
3) I have to talk with my boss/spouse/person in charge.
4) The competition has a better price or better product.
5) I've had bad experiences in the past.

These objections are natural parts of the sales process. The remaining type of objections are informative objections.

Generally, informative objections are easily handled if you know your product well. They're objections about the operation, characteristics, and results that a product or service promises. They are objections related to the product or industry, and therefore you'll know these answers better than anyone (I hope).

Objections natural to the sales process require a different approach. These objections require the salesman to know the sale's context along with the true reason behind why they come about. The industry that you're in has no bearing on these objections; they come about due to the psychological process that a sale involves for the customer.

But before teaching you the process that will lead you to avoid or shoot down every single one of these objections, I have to ask you to read the 3 mistakes that a *Well-Tailored Suit* like you should never make.

Common Mistakes when Handling an Objection

1) Getting defensive.
   (Leave your ego out of negotiation!)
2) Invalidating or conflicting with your customer's opinion.
   (AGREE: You always have to agree with them)
3) Trash talking the competition.
   (This only speaks badly of you and of no one else)

Now you're ready. Next, you have a simple 3-step process that you can use to handle any type of objection. This process has been proven by hundreds of salesman in varying industries and is simpler than it seems.

How to avoid or shoot down an objection?

Step #1: Anticipate the objection.

Make a list of all the most common objections from your customers and elaborate a written sales pitch where you not only anticipate them, but you also make your customer admit or state aloud that they won't be objections when closing the deal.

Example –

The most common objections to selling timeshares:

   A) We don't like being tied down to one chain.
   B) We've had bad experiences in the past.

In this case, you should add the following instructions to your sales process, to anticipate and block that objection before it even comes about:

Exchange A: (We don't like being tied down to one chain).

YOU: "Mr. Smith, what type of hotels do you stay in when traveling?"

THEM: "Whatever's available, we always like to try something new."

YOU: "Perfect! That's important, especially with so much supply in the hotel industry. So, flexibility when traveling is important for you?"

THEM: "Yes, very much so. We don't like to commit to a single chain."

YOU: "I understand, me neither, it would be quite boring. However sir, just to understand correctly, if I were to show you something that was highly flexible, that let you choose amongst thousands of hotels, and that gave you a fun and unique experience, would you consider my product?"

THEM: "Of course. I have an open mind."

<u>Exchange B:</u> (We've had bad experiences in the past).

   A) YOU: "Mr. Smith, let me ask you, before meeting me today, what were your impressions about timeshares?"

        THEM: "No way! Horrible to be honest. We once went to a presentation in Orlando and it lasted 3 hours. In truth, we are only here because we've been well received up until now, but we don't intend to buy."

        YOU: "I understand, Mr. Smith. Unfortunately there are a lot of companies out there whose sales processes aren't the best... And I'd never speak badly of my competitors! There actually are some excellent timeshares in Orlando, but that's the case in every industry. What is it that you do?

        THEM: "I'm a lawyer."

YOU: "You must be well aware of it then! The law is good, but there are lawyers who misuse it in not the best way and lawyers who use it terrifically, am I right?"

THEM: "Yes, it depends on the lawyer, the firm, or the company."

YOU: "The good thing is that you've already gotten to know the industry's "dark" side. And I couldn't be happier than to show you the excellent side. The side where service and wellbeing are priority.

Now, let me ask you something. If today I'm able to show you that my product is the best in the market and that it truly has the potential to change you and your family's life for the better, would you consider my product?"

THEM: "Of course, I just might."

Repeat this process with all of the most common objections that you have. At the beginning it will be tiring. You'll have to invest around an hour of your time to pinpoint every single objection and write out the exchange you'd like to have to anticipate them. But afterwards, these exchanges boil down to simple questions during your presentation, and you'll handle them automatically.

ACTION:

- Start using your anti-objection exchange list that will help you shoot them down before they even come about.

Step #2: Analyze your objections.

We've said it before: the difference between a good salesman and an outstanding salesman is how one reacts in the face of rejection.

It's in that moment of rejection, when the exchange is fresh in your memory, that you must take 5 minutes to analyze what your mistake was.

Analyze the objection that you couldn't handle. Or even better: call your boss, a colleague, or another salesman that you know to talk about your exchange and to analyze together what you could have done better to fight the objection.

ACTION:

- Carry a small black rejection book with you.

    Get yourself a black book and take note of every objection you get in a month. Use the book right after receiving the objection and take note of what would be the best response.

    Keep the book with you and utilize it to improve your answers.

To objectively analyze the objections, it's also important to know what the true meaning is behind every one of the natural objections to the sales process.

Objection #1: It's too expensive.

What does your customer really mean?

You haven't showed me that your product is worth what you're asking for.

What do you need to do?

Add value to your product. Make a list of all your product's benefits and find out ways to sell to your customers during your presentation. You need to justify the price you are asking for with value.

Objection #2: I need to think about it.

What does your customer really mean?

I don't trust you or your company and you haven't built up a sense of urgency. I'm in no hurry.

What do you need to do?

Give better service and build more rapport. Remember that you have to give to get. Try to build an emotional connection with your customer that creates strong bonds between you both along with personal credibility.

Create urgency! Use concepts like: limited stock, limited-time offer, the owners already have a buyer lined up, it's the last one available, etc., etc.

Objection #3: I need to talk with my boss/spouse/person in charge.

What does your customer really mean?

I need to talk with my boss/spouse/person in charge. (DUH!)

What do you need to do?

Speak with the person that really makes the decisions. Unfortunately, you just wasted energy and resources speaking to someone who doesn't have decision-making power.

To avoid this, improve your prospecting and make sure to be standing face to face with people that can make the decisions.

Objection #4: The competition has a better price or better product.

What does your customer really mean?

Again: You haven't showed me that your product is worth the price you're asking for.

What do you need to do?

NEVER compete on price. Add so much value to your product that deciding to go with you is the obvious choice and nearly obligatory.

Objection #5: I've had bad experiences in the past.

What does your customer really mean?

I've had bad experiences in the past, I'm nervous, I don't trust you, and I want to know if you are just like everybody else.

What do you need to do?

Show empathy for their bad experience and acknowledge that these situations exist, but not in your company! You must show them that you are different and the best option in the market.

Step #3: Sell on!

Do you know what the most difficult objection of all is?

The one you've never heard!

So sell on and write down every single one of them in your little black objection book, and be prepared to have to forget everything and improvise if necessary.

<u>Human beings are unpredictable… There's no roadmap!</u>

RECAP:

- There's two types of objections: the ones that are natural to the sales process and the informative ones. Both can be overcome.
- The process to shooting down an objection is: Anticipate, analyze, and sell on!
- Be prepared but stay flexible to change. Human beings are unpredictable and everything is at stake.

CHAPTER 40

Rejection: Your feelings to the blender

"Every time I thought I was being rejected from something good, I was actually being re-directed to something better."
- Dr. Steve Maraboli

Rejection, the second reason of why jobs in sales are so well-paid and the main reason for why only us madmen get into the industry.

Admit it, who likes to be told NO every day? Nobody!

Nonetheless, and as we've already discussed, the way you handle rejection, failure, and frustration will be key to turning you into a successful and consistent salesman.

Here you have my 4 best tips to getting dozens of those NO's and moving on with your chin held high.

TIP #1: Learn your closing rate!

Every industry has a different average closing rate. Learning the average closing rate for your product will give you a reference point and will keep you from getting frustrated at not closing 100% of your deals.

As a recommendation, always shoot to produce 30% more than the average closing rate for your product or industry. If you shoot high, at worst you'll fall somewhere in average and with lots of drive you'll be #1.

If you have the good fortune of selling in teams, never compare your numbers to your best buddy Bill's, who started selling fake Rolexes in the sales room for a bit of extra cash.

Compare yourself with the best closer. With the guy that sells every day and never wastes their time on anything other than producing large quantities of money. We are the average of the people we surround ourselves with. Surround yourself with people that motivate you to be better.

TIP #2: See it like it is – An opportunity to learn.

There's nothing closer to success than failure. When you fall down and get up, you're only climbing up one more step on the path towards your personal goals (even if it seems just the opposite). Accept that making mistakes is human. And most importantly: Analyze what you did wrong and what you could do better next time. Never waste an opportunity to learn from your mistakes.

The mere fact of talking about your mistakes and telling word for word what happened to someone you respect (and *please* someone who is successful in sales), turns a mistake into an opportunity to learn. Don't let your ego get in the way; even if you have been closing deals for 30 years, you'll always have something to learn; a new pitch, a new way of preventing or dismantling an objection, a new technology tool that solves your customers' problems – We never stop learning.

We live in a world that punishes mistakes as if it weren't part of our nature and the most basic element of our learning process. Don't be afraid to make mistakes, but grow with each mistake. Kick the stone aside, and never trip over it again.

<u>TIP #3: Don't have time to feel bad. Sell on!</u>

Analyze for a moment: When do you feel bad about not selling? During the sale? Before the sale? Or in your downtime? If your answer is during or before, there's your problem: You're kicking off and driving through your sale with the wrong attitude.

During your presentation you can't think about ANYTHING else than how much you're going to sell and about how happy your customer will be with what you're selling them. Sales are jealous, and if they don't have 100% of your energy, 100% of your positive attitude and attention – meaning – if you have a plan B or one foot out of the equation… You're not going to make the sale.

If your answer is "In my downtime" …. Easy: Don't have downtime! Sell away! Remember that if you aren't being told no, you're not selling enough.

You've got 4 hours before your next meeting? That's your problem! Apply those 4 hours to getting more, to reading a book about sales, to watching a motivational video, to listening to courses on your iPhone or even to playing with your family and relaxing. Occupy your time with something positive, productive, and beneficial!

And don't self-sabotage. Making mistakes is human. Accept it and <u>MOVE ON.</u>

And the last tip:

<u>TAKE IT PERSONALLY!</u>

Contrary to many sales managers' philosophy of "don't worry about it, don't take it personal," you have to do exactly the opposite. Take each NO completely personally. If you were indifferent to rejection, something would be wrong with you and you would never build up enough drive and energy to analyze each case and learn from it.

Every outstanding salesperson aspires to a single philosophy on how to handle rejection.

An outstanding salesperson divorces their ego and self-esteem from the NO's they receive day to day.

An outstanding salesperson knows that the prospect isn't attacking your person. The prospect is defending their money tooth and nail (just as the salesperson would do).

An outstanding salesperson knows that their own mind is their best tool and worst enemy, and knows when not to listen to it.

An excellent salesperson never stops selling.

RECAP:

- Making mistakes is part of human nature. Accept it, learn from your mistakes, and don't trip over the same stone twice.
- Learn your closing rate and set realistic goals!
- Don't have time to feel bad… Sell on!
- Take it personally!

ACTION:

- Start using these tips RIGHT AWAY!

Somewhere, take note of these 4 tips and re-read them at the moment you feel most distracted by the last NO you received. I promise you this article will raise your chin up high again.

CHAPTER 41

The Most Important Part of a Sale

> *"A.B.C.: Always be closing."*
> *- Blake, Glengarry Glen Ross*

Which is it? Which is the most important part of a sale?

It truly is hard to decide, since sales are like football or like an industrial kitchen during lunch rush, if one of the parts isn't doing its job right, we're not going to score a touchdown; we're not going to feed all those hungry people out there.

As you've seen up until now, being a salesman has many parts, elements, and things to take into consideration. Selling is half art, half science, and half chaos. Being an outstanding salesman is a combination of persuasive personality with heavy-duty internal motivation and very good preparation.

But I still wonder… Which is the most important part of a sale?

And I arrive at two answers. I can't decide on just one.

I see my options and I go for these two:

Service and "the question."

Selling is about service, if you serve a customer, an industry, and a community, in turn, they'll serve you.

Service adds value, grants humility, inspires respect, creates compassion, friendship, and all of the planet's positive energy.

Service makes the perfect sale. Service creates an eternally happy customer and a 0% cancelation rate.

Service honestly rendered and an outstanding smile is key to selling in the long run.

And the question, the question is so primal that it's illogical how it's the reason most sales and businesses get away from you.

It's the question that an underprepared salesman is terrified to ask.

The question that you'll only feel comfortable asking whenever you've done outstanding work. But even when you feel that your work wasn't the best, you still have to make yourself ask it if you intend to sell.

The famous question:

"And how would you like to pay, sir? Cash, Visa, or MasterCard?

RECAP:

- Service is key to making the perfect sale.
- Never stop asking "And how would you like to pay, sir?"

ACTION:

- Sell away, growing and enhancing the name of the industry. Turn yourself into a salesman who inspires, wearing the highest quality Well-Tailored Suit.

WHO IS CRIS URZUA?

Licensed in Marketing, salesman and author who's terrified of mediocrity.

Leader with years of experience training salesforces from government companies responsible for volumes over $15 million dollars per year.

Founder of Mindset and Skills Acdemy and of the flagship course for salespeople SellingThroughService™

Current trainer, Sales conference speaker, writer, and digital entrepreneur.

Learn more at:

www.crisurzua.com .

www.mindsetandskills.com

www.sellingthroughservice.com

GLOSSARY

Hawaiian Shirts: Term referring to mediocre and unethical salespeople.

Well-tailored Suits: Term referring to successful, ethical, highly service-oriented salespeople, who add value and have attention to detail.

Pitch: Offer, referring to the words or writing that one follows during preparation for a sales presentation.

Base Reality: Referring to the reality holding no regard on human volition. The most basic blocks of our existence: breathing, eating, sleeping, etc.

Capital Reality: Referring to the reality that does indeed bear regard to human volition. They are our consumerist, capitalist, and self-realization aspirations.

RECAP: A section from each chapter where the most important points are summarized.

ACTION: A section of mandatory exercises from each of the book's chapters.

GOODIES: Freebies, referring to the chapter section containing a free gift.

Everybody Sells

Escape from Mediocrity, Close Every One of your Sales, and Live and Epic Life.

Written by Cris Urzua

www.crisurzua.com

www.mindsetandskills.com

www.sellingthroughservice.com

#Everybody Sells

© *Cris Urzua 2015*

Translated by Matthew James Roudebush from MJR Languages, Lima, Peru.

Contact@MJRLanguages.com
Facebook.com/MJRLanguage
www.MJRLanguages.com

www.ingramcontent.com/pod-product-compliance
Lightning Source LLC
Chambersburg PA
CBHW050057230526
45470CB00004B/1569